TEN SERMONS
on the
SECOND ADVENT

TEN SERMONS
on the
SECOND ADVENT

E. W. BULLINGER

kregel
PUBLICATIONS

Grand Rapids, MI 49501

Ten Sermons on the Second Advent by E. W. Bullinger

Published by Kregel Publications, a division of Kregel, Inc., P.O. Box 2607, Grand Rapids, MI 49501. Kregel Publications provides trusted, biblical publications for Christian growth and service. Your comments and suggestions are valued.

Cover photograph: Image Club Photogear vol. 6
Cover and book design: Alan G. Hartman

Library of Congress Cataloging-in-Publication Data

Bullinger, E. W. (Ethelbert William), 1837–1913.
   Ten sermons on the Second Advent /
by E. W. Bullinger.
      p.   cm.
   1. Second Advent—Sermons. 2. Sermons, English.
3. Dispensationalism—Sermons. I. Title.
BT886.B85   1996   236'.9—dc20   95-24908
                                    CIP

ISBN 0-8254-2162-4 (pbk.)

1 2 3 4 5 printing / year 00 99 98 97 96

Printed in the United States of America

CONTENTS

CHAPTER 1

THE IMPORTANCE OF PROPHETIC STUDY

We have also a more sure word of prophecy; whereunto ye do well that ye take heed (as unto a light that shineth in a dark place, until the day dawn, and the day star arise) in your hearts (2 Peter 1:19, parentheses mine).

However unimportant the study of prophecy may be in the judgment of men, we learn from our text that it is a subject of the greatest importance in the sight of God.

It is true that the great majority of professing Christians dismiss prophecy as being unimportant and uninteresting. This may be because instead of allowing God to mean what He says, each interpreter declares that He means something very different. Thus, the ordinary Bible reader is bewildered with the Babel about it. It may be that the belief that Christ will not come until at least a thousand years makes it useless to look for Him or to study the Scriptures that speak of His return. It may also be that the belief that Christ comes at the death of each believer renders it a matter of little consequence whether He will return before or after the Millennium.

Hence when one and another raises the midnight cry, Behold the Bridegroom cometh, it is treated as the warning of Lot was treated when he seemed as one that mocked unto his sons-in-law.

They are confessedly ignorant of the subject and this doubtless is the reason of their confidence that the prophecies are unprofitable, if not dangerous.

But we are to consider this great subject together because we believe in the importance of the sure word of prophecy; our object is to have this importance impressed on our hearts.

Let us first consider the place which God Himself has given it in His Word. Our aim ought ever to be to hold all truth in proportion, for truth out of proportion becomes error. Not only must we receive God's truth because it is the truth, but we must receive it in the order in which God has revealed it, in the proportion in which God has given it, and with the emphasis that God has put upon it.

Now look at prophetic truth in this light. What was the very first promise in Eden? Was it not a prophecy concerning the seed of the woman and His victory over that old serpent the Devil? What did the faith of the patriarchs rest on but the word of prophecy? Abel's was faith in the coming sacrifice, Enoch's was faith in the coming Lord, Noah's was faith in a coming judgment, Abraham's was faith in a coming heir and a coming inheritance, Isaac's was faith in things to come, Jacob's was faith in a coming blessing, Joseph's was faith in a coming exodus, Moses' in a coming recompense of reward, while all looked and waited for some better thing and the better resurrection. Their faith was based on the sure word of prophecy. In the strength of faith in this, they suffered and they overcame.

The Pentateuch is filled with prophetic word and type. The ceremonial law, the tabernacle, and its ordinances were all shadows of good things to come.

The Psalms are full of the testimony of Jesus which is the spirit of prophecy. Of David we read that "he being a prophet"—"he seeing this before," spoke of Christ.

And besides the Psalms, there are seventeen books (out of thirty-nine) directly and wholly prophetic.

If we come to the New Testament we find that there are

260 chapters, and in them, what one other truth or doctrine will you find mentioned, as this is, 318 times?

If we take verses instead of chapters, we find one verse in every twenty-five referring to this great doctrine.

If we take its separate parts, we find that prophecy formed the one subject of John the Baptist's ministry, that the discourses of our Lord were permeated with prophecy, that nearly all the epistles contain prophecy, and that the last book in the Bible is nothing but prophecy.

As to ourselves, all our hopes are built on prophecy. The promise of future victory, the pledge of resurrection, the joys of heaven, the hope of glory, and all that we know about them is nothing but prophecy.

Surely, if we may judge of the importance of a doctrine by the prominence given to it in the Word of God, then we may say that we have in prophecy a subject whereunto you do well that you take heed in your hearts.

If we need an example as to our proper attitude with reference to it, we have only to look at Daniel. God had made him a prince among prophets. As a scholar, a statesman, and a saint, he was preeminent. He was a man greatly beloved and highly favored, with no howbeit! Well, how did he treat the word of prophecy? Jeremiah had preceded him and foretold the captivity of his people in Babylon. Did Daniel say it did not concern him? That it was not important? No! He did well and took heed in his heart to the word of prophecy: "I Daniel understood by books the number of the years, whereof the word of the LORD came to Jeremiah the prophet, that he would accomplish seventy years in the desolations of Jerusalem" (Dan. 9:2). What was the effect of his prophetic study? See the next verses, "And I set my face unto the Lord God . . . and I prayed unto the LORD my God." The study of prophecy drew him to his God and laid him at His feet. The same may be said of Simeon. He was among those who were waiting for the consolation of Israel, and the Holy Ghost was upon him. He found his rest in Christ as God's salvation "prepared" to be "a light to lighten the Gentiles, and the glory of thy people Israel" (Luke 2:25–32). The same may be said of Anna. She was among those who looked for redemption in Jerusalem. This looking drew her very near to the Redeemer, for He was the burden of her testimony—she "spake of him" (Luke 2:38). These saints had been diligent students of prophecy, and God honored them both by a vision of Him for whom they had waited and looked.

Yes, Jesus is the spirit of prophecy, and no study of it can be right that does not lead to and end in Him. You may see the effect of mere head knowledge in "the chief priests and scribes" (Matt. 2). They knew the letter of prophecy. When Herod demanded of them where Christ would be born, they could take the sacred roll and put their finger on Micah 5:2, where Micah prophesied that out of Bethlehem should come the "Governor" (see Matt. 2:6). But there it ended. They had no love for that Governor, while the wise men, truly wise though ignorant of the written Word, could not rest until they found their place in worship at His feet. Thus those who had mere head knowledge (that only "puffeth up") placed that knowledge at the service of Herod to compass the destruction of Jesus, while those who had true heart love (which "buildeth up") were divinely guided and found their happy place at Jesus' feet.

Surely we should not lightly esteem that part of God's Word to which we are specially exhorted to take heed in our hearts, and on which He has thus specially set His seal. Nor can it be right to speak of those who love His appearing as eccentric! Alas, that they are eccentric is only too true, but this only shows how far the bulk of professing Christians have drifted from the divine order and the divine importance of God's Word.

If this doctrine, which holds so large a place in the Bible, is neglected and unheeded by the majority of professing Christians, we need no other evidence that the church is departing from the faith and has entered on the downgrade.

If we were asked to name the subjects which are put forward today with the greatest frequency and urgency, we would say they are baptism and the Lord's Supper. But note the place that these occupy and the position given to them in the Epistles, which were written specially for the instruction of the church. Baptism is mentioned only nine-teen times in seven epistles (the noun five and the verb fourteen), and it is not once named in fourteen out of the twenty-one epistles. As for the Lord's Supper, there are not more than three or four references to it in the whole of the New Testament. In twenty (out of twenty-one) of the epistles it is never once alluded to! From the prominence given to it by man, one would imagine the New Testament to be filled with it. It is not a question of one subject being important and another not. It is a question of proportion and relation. Certainly if the Scriptures contain twenty references to the one subject of the Lord's coming, to one reference concerning another, we may say that God has settled for us what He deems profitable for us and important.

And is it nothing that the Father has revealed to us the things which He has prepared for them that love Him? Is it nothing that Jesus has assured us that He is coming to receive us into that place which He has gone to prepare for us? Is it nothing that the Holy Spirit has caused holy men of old to write these things for our learning and has been sent on purpose to guide us into all truth, and to show us things to come (John 16:12–13)? Alas, alas, the need for these questions shows us the character of the times and shows how the Enemy of the Word of God is succeeding in his one great object. What has been the great device of the Enemy from the very beginning until now? Has it not been to deny, pervert, and hide the Word of God? What was it that caused the overthrow of the old world? Disdain of the prophetic warnings of Noah! They thought prophecy was of no importance! But "As it was in the days of Noah . . . as it was in the days of Lot . . . even thus shall it be when the Son of man is revealed" (Luke 17:26–30, Matt. 24:37–39). Israel received warning after warning from God's inspired prophets, but it was of no importance, they thought; so people say today, but their end will be the same, and the word that God has spoken shall judge them in that day.

Note again the words of our text, "We have a more sure word of prophecy whereunto ye do well that ye take heed (as unto a light that shineth in a dark place, until the day dawn and the day star arise) in your hearts." I call your attention to the parenthesis in which I place this clause, and connect the words *take heed* with the words *in your hearts.* We have many examples of such parentheses in the Scriptures.[1]

Where this parenthesis is disregarded, the day dawn and day star rising in the heart is usually explained as meaning conversion. But this explanation infers that prophecy should be well heeded until conversion, and then it may be neglected. This clearly cannot be the meaning! The parenthesis must be observed if we would get any sense from this passage. No wonder that the verse should come to be taken as though it said prophecy is a dark place which ye do well to avoid! For people do call it dark indeed, and most certainly they avoid it. But the Holy Spirit describes this world as the dark place, and states that this word of prophecy is the only lamp in it; the only light that can show us where we are and whither all is tending.

Prophecy is the light that shines during this night (which, thank God, is "far spent") "until the day dawn and the shadows flee away," until that "morning without clouds," when the day star shall rise (Rev. 22:16). Then we shall have the True Light itself, of which the prophets did write.

Surely, if it is written, "whereunto ye do well that ye take heed," we do *not* well if we treat it as of little or no importance. Foreseeing all this the Holy Spirit has pronounced a solemn and emphatic blessing on all who obey the precept of our text: "Blessed is he that readeth, and they that hear the words of this prophecy, and keep those things which are written therein" (Rev. 1:3). He does not say anything about understanding it, but reading, hearing, and keeping it—in other words, taking heed to it in our hearts. It follows, therefore, that those who do not thus heed it must of necessity lose the promised blessing. Again it is written (2 Tim. 3:16–17), "All scripture is given by inspiration of God, and is profitable."[2] How many treat the Scripture as though it were not all profitable, as though one quarter at least were not profitable. They cannot believe that all Scripture is profitable without condemning their confessed neglect of so large a portion of it!

But it does not end with neglect, for while most neglect it, many pervert it, others merely speculate about it and treat what they call "prophetic language" according to their fancies and imaginations. They thus make the word of prophecy of none effect and put it to an open shame—not that this can form any excuse for our neglect of that Word, for this treatment of Scripture has characterized every age of ecclesiastical history.

What important truth or fundamental doctrine has not suffered from the follies of writers who have speculated and reasoned about spiritual truths? All through the ages people have been turned to fables and have given heed to wandering spirits and doctrines of demons. Hence the deity and atonement of Jesus, justification by grace, and nearly every other article of the Christian faith has been denied or perverted.

But surely this is all the greater reason why we should contend for them and take heed to them. If the great doctrine of the Second Advent of our Lord has been covered over and obscured with the teachings of men, there is all the more reason why we should seek to separate what God has said from what man has taught, and bend our devout and earnest attention the more earnestly to this great and important subject.

There is one other consideration that I might urge, if another be needed. Perhaps it is second to none in its powerful conclusions. It is the one that is to form the subject of our sixth sermon and therefore I need not do much more than mention it here. It is this: The importance of prophecy as seen in its practical effects on Christian life. The testimony of Jesus is the Spirit of prophecy, and therefore the right study of it necessarily links us with Jesus and occupies us with Him. Those who love Him will long for His appearing that they may see Him, and this longing will react and increase the love. We are exhorted to wait and watch for Him so that nothing may come between our hearts and Him, and that thus our characters may be formed.

"We beholding . . . are changed into the same image." No restless efforts, no anxious toiling, but simply "We beholding . . . are changed"!

Christian life is not molded by precepts or regulated by ordinances. The Law, which was holy, just, and good, only proved the impotence of the sinner in order that he might cast himself on the omnipotence of the Savior. Hence we find that the grace that brings salvation (Titus 2:11–14) also teaches us how to live and what to live for. The Law only commanded, but grace teaches and gives the ability to learn. It teaches us to look for that blessed hope and the glorious appearing of the great God and our Savior Jesus Christ who gave Himself for us.

If any fail to look for that blessed hope, it is clear that they either know nothing of the salvation that grace brings, or that they have not learned the lessons that grace teaches.

This view of the subject lifts it completely out of the region of mere theological strife and gives it its true position as the divine means for the formation of Christian character. It shows that it is quite as much a question of piety as it is of prophecy. And what is more, any theory or system of doctrine that has the effect of causing those who hold it not to look for that blessed hope, or not to wait for God's Son from heaven, is thus shown to be contrary to, and subversive of, the great lesson which grace teaches.

There are many books from which this lesson is omitted, but they are not divine. There are many sermons in which you never find it, but they are neither apostolic nor primitive. They are the outcome of fleshly wisdom and human learning, or the products of minds that do not believe that "all Scripture is . . . profitable," and that do not obey the injunction of our text.

Dear friends, may we give this great subject the place it ought to occupy in our minds, in our hearts, and in our lives. Remember that, after all, it depends not so much on wisdom in the head as on grace in the heart. It is a heart subject. See how it is thus presented in Titus 2:13–14: "Looking for that blessed hope, and the glorious appearing of the great God and our Savior Jesus Christ; *who gave himself for us"* (italics mine, and in 1 Thessalonians 5:9–10, speaking of waking or sleeping with reference to the appearing of Jesus, the apostle says: "for God hath not appointed us to wrath, but to obtain salvation by our Lord Jesus Christ, *who died for us,* that, whether we wake or sleep, we should live together with Him," and again in 1 Thessalonians 1:10, "To wait for His Son from heaven, whom He raised from the dead, *even Jesus who delivered us from the wrath to come."*

It has been said of a vast mountain that what is transcendently great seems constantly near. And we may say the same of this great doctrine. Oh, that this blessed hope may be ever great and ever near: great in its importance to our minds, great in its influence on our lives, and ever near in its preciousness to our hearts.

Endnotes

1. See Ephesians 1:19, "according . . . all in all," to end of chapter. Then 2:1 takes up the theme. So that it reads thus: 1:19, "And what is the exceeding greatness of his power to usward who believe," 2:1, "even you who were dead in trespasses and sins."

   See another illustration in Ephesians 3 (sermon no. 5).

   An important example is found in 1 Corinthians 15 where, if verses 20 to end of 28 are put into a parenthesis, the sense reads on thus—If there be no resurrection then they which are fallen asleep in Christ are perished, and in that case, what is the good of anyone being baptized into Christ to take the place of those who have only perished (this is the force of the word translated "for" see Rom. 5:6–8, Gal 2:20; Eph. 5:25; Philem. 13; Heb. 2:9; 1 Peter 2:21, etc., where it means "instead of," or "taking the place of").

   We ought to observe that these parentheses generally arise from introverted parallels in the structure of the originals, for example, Genesis 15:13, "Thy seed shall be a stranger in a land that is not theirs, and shall serve them; and they shall afflict them four hundred years."

2. The Revisers translate this, "Every Scripture inspired of God is also profitable," etc. But this is not English, to say nothing of the Greek. For it can no more be "Every Scripture" than Ephesians 2:21 can mean every building. The word *also* is meaningless unless a previous assertion has been made.

Hebrews 4:13 is strictly parallel in its structure and in the arrangement of the words, but the Revisers have emphasized the rendering of the KJV, "are naked and laid open," and have not said, "All things naked are also laid open"! Likewise in 1 Timothy 4:14, they have said, "Every creature of God is good and nothing is to be rejected," and have not said, "Every good creature of God is *also* nothing to be rejected"! Thus they themselves condemn their rendering of 2 Timothy 3:16.

CHAPTER 2

THE INTERPRETATION OF PROPHECY

Knowing this first, that no prophecy of the scripture is of any private interpretation. For the prophecy came not in old time [mg at any time] by the will of man: but holy men of God spake as they were moved by the Holy Ghost (2 Peter 1:20–21).

The words of the twentieth verse are confessedly difficult of translation, and have given rise to many and various interpretations. The Revisers, after we may suppose the fullest consideration, have adhered to the KJV, merely omitting the word *any*, and then giving verse 21, thus: "For no prophecy came (mg was brought) by the will of man: but men spake from God being moved by the Holy Ghost."

The difficulty arises partly from the fact that the word translated "interpretation" occurs nowhere else in the whole Bible (and only once or twice in secular writings). We have therefore to seek its meaning chiefly from the context. Even the verb from which this noun is formed occurs only twice in the New Testament (Mark 4:34 and Acts 19:39), and in the Old Testament only once (Gen. 41:12). Literally, it means a "loosening upon, unloosing," then, of what is before unknown, "an unfolding." Hence the rendering "interpretation."

Then, the word "private" is the translation of a Greek

word that occurs 112 times and is never translated "private" except in this verse! Seventy-two times it is rendered "his own," for example, his own sheep, his own city, his own brother, his own place, his own body, and so forth.

But no translation of this verse can be correct that does not allow the verb its full and proper force. The verb here translated "is," is no part of the ordinary verb to be; it is another verb altogether, and means "to begin to be, to come into existence, to originate, to produce, to become."

Now, putting these facts together and remembering that the next verse begins with *for* ("for the prophecy," etc.), thus depending on and flowing from verse 20, we arrive at the following sense: "Knowing this first that no prophecy of the Scripture came originated] of his [the prophet's] own unfolding, for no prophecy ever came by the will of man, but men spake from God [not from themselves] moved by the Holy Ghost."

Prophecy is the unfolding of the future, and though men were used as instruments, they did not originate or produce it of themselves. It came from God, by His Holy Spirit.

This being so, prophecy comes to us already as an interpretation of the future. Our business with it is not so much to interpret this interpretation as to receive and believe the interpretation that it gives to us. The same Holy Spirit who inspired the prophecy is now with the church of Christ, and His special mission is to unfold the Scriptures to us. "He will guide you into all truth . . . and he will show you things to come" (John 16:13–14). Speaking of the natural man, it is written: "Eye hath not seen, nor ear heard, neither have entered into the heart of man, the things which God hath prepared for them that love him. But God hath revealed them unto us by his Spirit" (1 Cor. 2:9–10).

David was a prophet, and in 2 Samuel 23:1–3 we read, "David the son of Jesse, *said* . . . the sweet psalmist of Israel *said*, 'The Spirit of the Lord *spake* by me and his word was in my tongue. The God of Israel *said*, the Rock of Israel *spake* to me'" (italics mine). It is not possible to emphasize the truth of our text more strongly, and we have here a wonderful corroboration of its truth and importance.

Prophecy therefore (and in this statement the whole Bible is of course included) did not originate from any private views, peculiar ideas, or favorite theories of any men. It is divine, and no matter how intelligent, or scholarly, any student of prophecy may be, he must have the illumination of the Spirit of God. Artificial light may reveal the beauties of the structure of a sundial and display its carvings or mosaics or outward design, but only heaven's light can show heaven's time. So the natural wisdom of man may see many beauties in the geography, history, antiquities, and language of the Bible, but only heaven's wisdom can give heaven's mind, for "the natural man receiveth not the things of the Spirit of God; for they are foolishness unto him; neither can he know them because they are spiritually discerned" (1 Cor. 2:14). Scholarship may understand the written letter, but only the man who is taught of the Spirit who gave the prophecy can grasp its meaning. It is as true today as when God said it by David: "The secret of the Lord is with them that fear him and he will show them his covenant (mg *and His covenant to make them to know it*)" (Ps. 25:14). Such a one shall know about the teaching. The student of prophecy needs a more thorough equipment than any that mere efficient scholarship or biblical criticism can give. The highest gifts must be sanctified by the divine interpreter Himself.

When any person or any church assumes this prerogative of the Holy Spirit, the claim to infallibility is the logical sequence of such an assumption. This, therefore, is the great, first, and important point. "Knowing this first," says the Holy Spirit by Saint Peter, "that no prophecy of the Scripture came from the prophet's own interpretation."

It is remarkable and interesting to note that the two men who stand out in the Old Testament as interpreters of dreams and visions sent from God, Joseph and Daniel, both pointedly emphasize this truth. Joseph said to Pharaoh, when asked to make known the future revealed in the dream, "It is not in me: God shall give Pharaoh an answer of peace" (Gen. 41:16); Daniel said to Nebuchadnezzar, "He that revealeth secrets maketh known to thee what shall

come to pass, but as for me, this secret is not revealed to me
for any wisdom that I have more than any living" (Dan.
2:29–30).

The subject before us is purely a subject of revelation.
Outside of this blessed Book we know absolutely nothing
of the future. The world is dark, and this Book is the only
light in it. Speculation, imagination, reason, and philoso-
phy have no part nor lot here; they have no value whatever
in answering the question, What is truth. There would be
no difficulty in having a Bible exactly according to our own
minds if each one might set up his own reason as the standard as to what is likely to be or what God is likely to do.
That is just how people are everywhere acting. But that is
not what settles questions revealed in this Book. This Book
claims to be from God. It claims to make known His
thoughts and to reveal His will and purposes. The men
who wrote it wrote down not what they imagined or pre-
sumed to reason out, not what they thought would prove
acceptable to others, not what they themselves might deem
wise or think beneficent, but they wrote down what God
thought, what God chose to say, what God commanded, yes
and what God *meant!* Holy men spoke from God. What our
attitude ought to be, therefore, is perfectly clear, and our
duty is very simple: to accept what they reveal as the truth
of God. We have no option whatever, no right of debate or
appeal, as to things revealed. We are merely like students
who sit down to study the statutes of the Realm. The one
and only question is, what do they say? No matter whether
we can understand them, explain them, or harmonize them
with our own views or with the views of others. Our duty
as students is to know them, and as citizens, to obey them.

So these Holy Scriptures reveal what God pleases to say.
Our duty is to accept and believe them because of that, and
not because of our ability to understand them. The one
great difficulty is that the authority of Scripture is not
regarded as absolutely supreme. So long as people insist on
squaring Scripture with reason, so long can there be no certainty in the things of faith. There can be no unity of doctrine unless there be first a unity of authority. We have no

more to do, and no less, than Israel had when Moses came forth from God, and down from Horeb, and made known what God had written and revealed.

We, therefore, have not to interpret revelation, because revelation is given to interpret to us what we otherwise could never have known. This must be our ground and this our spirit in approaching the word of prophecy. This must be our foundation. The deeper and the firmer this is laid, the higher may be the superstructure that we build upon it; whereas, a lofty structure erected on a feeble foundation must end in ruin and disaster.

If God has not made known to us things to come, then we can never know them. But if He has, then we need not be ignorant.

Now we shall not deny that this revelation uses sometimes figures of speech and symbols, types, and visions (though I believe that where a symbol is used, the explanation is generally given by the divine Spirit Himself). But if it be impossible to distinguish between the figurative language and the literal facts of which that language speaks, then we have no revelation at all: we have an apocrypha; we have concealment; we have something as useless and as ambiguous as the oracles of the heathen. If there be anything in the language of Scripture that is figurative, that is one thing. To assert (as many people do) that the thing itself of which the language speaks is also figurative, that is quite another thing.

Now, to pass on; we all confess that the prophecies concerning Christ's first advent were fulfilled to the letter. Indeed we all base a powerful argument in favor of the inspiration of the Bible on this fact. If you search the Scriptures you will find 109 such predictions literally fulfilled at Christ's first advent in the flesh. The place of His birth; His conception, lowly life, miracles, rejection, and betrayal; the smiting; the spitting, scourging, and piercing; the parting of the garments and casting lots for His vesture; the vinegar, the gall; His death and burial; His resurrection and ascension *all literally fulfilled!* Why then, when we read of His descension from heaven (2 Thess. 4:16), should we apply a canon of interpretation totally opposite and say that all is figurative?

Both advents rest on the same authority. Surely, if we accept that authority, it is no harder to understand it concerning what is to be than it is to believe it concerning what was to be. Both alike in their turn are contrary to human thoughts and occasions of stumbling to human reasoning. How do we know that Jesus was born, suffered, died, and rose again? Simply because we read it in the Word of God. Then, on precisely that same Word we know the circumstances connected with His coming again.

Having spoken of the authority of Scripture, let us now look at its language. For inspiration is the source of the authority, that authority is the basis of all knowledge, and the channel of this knowledge is language. The revelation is clothed in words. Once admit that words do not mean what they say, but something else and something different, then all the various schools of theological thought and every individual in those schools may spiritualize in opposite directions to suit their own views.

Unless God means exactly what He says according to the laws of all language, then all positive lines of demarcation between truth and error on all the vital verities of Christianity are at that moment obliterated. It is not merely the prophecies of the Second Advent that suffer, but all doctrines and all the articles of the Christian faith are involved in one common chaos.

Look now at a few examples showing how the language and the words of divine revelation are treated by this army of spiritualizers and figurative interpreters, who will not allow God to mean what He says and hardly to have a meaning for anything He says!

All the creeds of Christendom, ancient and modern, with hundreds of Scriptures, proclaim the fact concerning Christ—He shall come again.

But see in what different ways interpreters deal with this prophecy—

1. They assert that the coming of the Holy Spirit at Pentecost fulfills it.

But it is surely sufficient to observe that both the coming of the Holy Spirit and the coming again of Christ were foretold, and the one has been literally fulfilled. Surely then the inference is that the other will be. Again, in many instances the Holy Spirit and the Savior are emphatically distinguished in one and the same Scripture: "It is expedient for you that I go away; for if I go not away the Comforter will not come unto you: but if I depart I will send him unto you" (John 16:7). The coming of the Holy Spirit is supplementary to the first coming of Christ and preparatory to His second coming. How then can the coming of the Spirit take the place of the second any more than of the first? It will not do to shift the ground and say that a larger outpouring of the Spirit is meant because in no sense could the act of coming be a proper figure of a mere increase.

Those who thus spiritualize can have but a very vague idea of the mission of the Holy Spirit in this world during this dispensation, or of the sad dishonor they thus bring upon His wondrous work.

It must not be forgotten that hundreds of references to the Lord's second advent were inspired after Pentecost, and this fact alone forms an insuperable barrier against such a violation of the letter of Scripture.

2. Others say that the destruction of Jerusalem by Titus fulfills the prophecy.

This interpretation rests on Matthew 24, Mark 13, and Luke 21. In the fourth sermon we shall thoroughly examine these Scriptures and their mutual relation. It is sufficient for us to observe now that while they overlap in certain places, Matthew 24 contains no reference to the destruction of Jerusalem but enlarges on the events that immediately precede the coming of the Son of Man. Saint Luke epitomizes these events in four verses (8–11) and then (12–24) enlarges on the destruction of Jerusalem which he says shall be "before all these things," and then (v. 25) unites with Saint Matthew in speaking of the coming of Christ after the "times of the Gentiles be fulfilled." But in no sense does Matthew refer to Titus and his armies when he speaks of "the Son of man coming in the clouds of heaven with power and great glory" (Matt. 24:30). For when standing before Pilate, Jesus repeats the very same words (Matt. 26:64). Can it be that He spoke of Titus! At any rate His enemies did not so understand Him, for up to this point the evidence had been conflicting and the witness contradictory, but on uttering these words, the case was closed, their clothes were rent, and they pronounced Him guilty, worthy of death!

3. Others say that a spiritual coming of Christ now fulfills the prophecy.

Thank God, there is a spiritual presence of Christ now by His Spirit, for "where two or three are gathered together," or scattered abroad to the "uttermost parts of the earth," the promise holds good, "I am with you" (Matt. 28:20). But surely more than this is meant when it was written that "this same Jesus which is taken up from you into heaven shall so come in like manner as ye have seen him go into heaven" (Acts 1:11). Surely something more is in store for the church and for the world when we read that "times of refreshing shall come from the presence of the Lord and he shall send Jesus Christ which before was preached unto you: whom the heaven must receive until the times of restitution of all things" (Acts 3:20–21). Surely there is a definite interval between the taking up and the coming; between the heaven receiving and the Father sending! Yes, the promise of this interval is, I will come again; the ordinance of this interval is, Till He come; the command is, Occupy till I come; and the prayer is, Even so come Lord Jesus, Thy kingdom come.

4. Lastly, it is urged that the death of believers satisfies the prophecy.

So common is this belief that it has well-nigh blotted out the resurrection and the Advent as a hope, as the hope of the church. Jesus said, as words of greatest comfort to bereaved ones, "thy brother shall rise again," but the popular notion of death renders resurrection as unmeaning as it is unnecessary, and hence many spiritualize the references to it (especially in Rev 20:46). Like Hymeneus and Philetus, they say it is passed already, and "err concerning the faith" (2 Tim. 2:17–18). Jesus said, "I will come again," but the popular notion of death practically replies: No, Lord, I shall die and come to you! Thus there is no need and no room for the fulfillment of this and many other promises; no need to wait and watch and long for that coming; no need to desire to be among those that shall be alive and remain. No! This interpretation dislocates the Scripture and destroys the blessed hope that it presents. In Scripture, death is represented as an "enemy"—the last enemy, the great enemy (1 Cor. 15:26; Jer. 31:15); as a prison house (Job 3:17–18); as a sleep (Deut. 31:16; Job 14:2; Eccl. 9:10; Ps. 115:17; John 11:11). It will not be until our resurrection at the personal coming of Christ that our song shall be "O death, where is thy sting, O grave, where is thy victory." "Then," it says, "shall this saying be brought to pass" (1 Cor. 15:54–55). It is when we shall be "clothed upon" with our resurrection bodies that "mortality shall be swallowed up of life" (2 Cor. 5:4). It was only of a risen one that it was said, "He is not here" (Matt. 28:6). When Jesus said of John, "If I will that he tarry till I come," "this saying went abroad among the brethren that that disciple should not die," which showed their belief that to tarry until Jesus comes means not to die at all (John 21:22–23). And this is just what the Scripture teaches. It says, "We shall not all sleep" (1 Cor. 15:1); it says that those who shall be "alive and that are left" to the coming of the Lord "shall in no wise precede them that are fallen asleep." This passage teaches that it is only by resurrection (or translation) and ascension that we can enter heaven. "For since we believe that Jesus died and rose again, even so, through Jesus, God will bring [that is, bring again from the dead as He brought the Great Shepherd of the sheep, Heb. 13:20] with him those who have fallen asleep" (1 Thess. 4:14–15, RV). At least one generation of Christians shall never die at all, but shall be changed at the appearing of Christ our Life. This explains the words of Jesus in John 11:25–26, "I am the resurrection, and the life: he that believeth in me, though he were dead, (RV *die*) yet shall he live." To him I am the Resurrection, and whosoever liveth (that is, is alive at My coming) and believeth on Me, shall never die. To him I am the Life! And "when Christ, who is our life shall appear, then shall ye also appear with him in glory" (Col. 3:4).

Now let us pass on to look at the actual words employed by the Holy Spirit.

1. The word that is Englished *apocalypse*. It means "a removal of the vail from," so that what was before hidden may be seen. It occurs nineteen times and is translated "revelation," fourteen times; "manifestation," once; "appearing," once; "coming," once; and "to lighten," once, so that "revelation" is the proper meaning, and indeed no other Greek word is so translated in the New Testament. Whenever it is used of persons, it always requires their visible presence. There are only two apparent exceptions. One is Galatians 1:15–16, "When it pleased God . . . to reveal his Son in me." *In* when used of time, always means "on" or "upon," and the apostle is referring to the time of his conversion. All three accounts of it speak of a personal appearance of Christ which constituted his claim to apostleship: "last of all He was seen of me also as of one born out of due time" (1 Cor. 15:8). The other is Matthew 11:27, "Neither knoweth any man the Father, save the Son and he to whom the Son will reveal him." But this is no exception, for Jesus Himself by His personal presence did reveal the Father, as He said, "he that hath seen me hath seen the Father" (John 14:9).

2. The word that is Englished *epiphany*. It means "manifestation by personal appearance" and is translated "appearing," five times, and "brightness," once. It is used, in every case except one, of His second advent. This exception, however, proves the rule because it refers to His first advent, which all agree was personal. "The grace which is now made manifest by the epiphany of our Savior Jesus Christ" (2 Tim. 1:9–10, author's paraphrase). The use of the verb throws still clearer light upon it (see Acts 27:20). "When neither sun nor stars in many days were epiphanized" (author's paraphrase). The context of every passage renders impossible every sense except the literal.

3. The word *parousia*, which means "presence." It occurs twenty-four times and is translated "coming," twenty-two times, and "presence," twice. Seventeen of these refer to the Second Advent. And here again the exceptions prove the rule. First Corinthians 16:17, "I am glad of the coming of Stephanas and Fortunatus and Achaicus: for that which was lacking on your part they have supplied." It is clear that if Christ's coming is figurative so must the coming of these be; if these men were bodily present with the apostle, and their help substantial, so must the presence of Christ be. Second Corinthians 7:6–7, "God . . . comforted us by the coming of Titus; and not by his coming only but, by the consolation wherewith he was comforted in you." And 2 Corinthians 10:10, "his bodily presence is weak." In all these cases it is indeed *bodily presence*. The word marks the moment when absence ceases and presence begins and sets forth therefore very powerfully the future, real, personal, and glorious coming and presence of our blessed Lord.

Look further at other words which qualify and define the promises of His coming.

1. "This same Jesus, which is taken up from you into heaven, shall so come in like manner as ye have seen him go into heaven" (Acts 1:11). How emphatic are the words, *this same;* not another, not His influences, not Titus and his armies, not death, but Jesus.

2. "The Lord himself shall descend from heaven" (1 Thess. 4:16), not the angels, not an archangel, but the Lord Himself.

3. The words "once" and "the second" in Hebrews 9:28 are conclusive. "Christ was once offered to bear the sins of many; and unto them that look for him shall he appear the second time." All the words, and even the smallest words, protest against any figurative interpretation. All the actions and verbs point to the same conclusion. They are all acts requiring the presence of a person to perform and accomplish them. The dead in Christ are to be raised, the living saints are to be changed, judgment is to be administered, and false Christs are to appear. Unless all these things are figurative then all the prophecies of Christ's coming must

be understood in the plain, literal sense in which a child would understand them. They were not given by anyone's unfolding, nor by or for anyone's interpretation. They are God's own interpretation of what would be else unknown to us, and they are to be received in their plain, grammatical sense with childlike simplicity and faith.

In sermon number 7 we shall consider the wondrous covenants made by God with Abraham and David. To them, these covenants were prophecies. How did they understand them? Literally! The oath concerning them was, "My covenant will I not break, nor alter the thing that is gone out of my lips" (Ps. 89:34). But this is what man dares to do! In reading the part fulfillment of the covenant in Luke 1:31–33, man does not hesitate to interpret half of it literally and the other half figuratively, so as to make it accord with his reason. His name was indeed "called Jesus," but as to His reigning over the house of Jacob on the throne of His father David, that is carnal, that is unreasonable, that is unlikely, and therefore man sits in judgment on God and alters the thing that is gone out of His lips!

While we thank God that He has given us such an abundance of exceeding great and precious promises, let us remember that He has said concerning them, "these are the true sayings of God." "Hath he said and shall he not do it."

Among His last words, He said (John 14:1–3), "If I go . . . I will come again, and receive you unto myself." "If I go," meant literally going; and so "I will come again," must mean literally coming. May we not repeat His own sure words, "If it were not so, I would have told you"? He has not so told us, and therefore it must be true. His very last word from heaven, closing up all revealed truth, confirms and ratifies all His many promises, "Surely I come quickly," and if we have not ceased to expect Him, or ceased to desire Him, our eager, heartfelt response will be, "Even so, come, Lord Jesus."

CHAPTER 3

THE SECOND ADVENT PREMILLENNIAL

The earth shall be full of the knowledge of the LORD, as the waters cover the sea (Isa. 11:9).

As the days of Noah were, so shall also the coming of the Son of man be (Matt. 24:37).

It is a fundamental article of the Christian faith that Jesus, who was conceived of a virgin, born in Bethlehem, suffered and died for the sins of His people, rose again from the dead, and ascended up into heaven, shall in due time come again with power and great glory. Whatever views individuals may hold concerning this event, all creeds and confessions of faith, Roman Catholic, Protestant, Western, and Oriental bear their witness to it; all the churches of the world can unite in the words of the Te Deum, "We believe that Thou shalt come to be our Judge."

Again, all are agreed that the Scriptures reveal a time of universal blessedness as being in store for this world, and the world itself looks forward to "a good time coming." All are agreed that it will be characterized by a universal knowledge of divine truth, universal subjection to divine rule, universal peace among nations, and blessing for "all

Israel." This happy period of the world is commonly spoken of by the word *millennium* (two Latin words which together mean "a thousand years"), because five times in six verses (Rev. 20:1–6) when Saint John speaks of that age, he calls it "a thousand years."

Now while all Christians are agreed as to these two great facts: (1) that Christ is coming, and (2) that this time of universal blessedness is also coming, yet all are not agreed as to the relation of these two events, the one to the other. The simple question is this, which of these two events will take place first?

The question is not whether Christ is coming and it is not whether a Millennium of peace is coming, but which of these events precedes the other.

All other questions in connection with the Second Advent are subordinate to this, because if Christ is to come first, then there can be no hope of improvement in or blessing for the world until Christ comes; it is both foolish and vain to look and labor for it. And, if the Millennium is to come first, then it is equally vain to be constantly looking for that blessed hope and waiting and watching for Christ.

In the early ages of the church, Christians looked for Christ to come first and the word *millenarian* was sufficient to describe them. When some began to look for the Millennium to come first, it became necessary to make an addition to this word, and hence those who looked for Christ to come first were called *premillenarians*. Those who looked for the Millennium to come first were called *postmillenarians*, but the primitive church knew nothing of these terms, for postmillennial views were unknown and unheard of.

The early Christians looked for Christ. They waited for God's Son from heaven. They looked for a person, and not for a Millennium without Him. It has been reserved for a later generation to place the Millennium before the church, as its hope.

Now to make the point still more clear let me repeat that premillennialists look for Christ to come before the thousand years; postmillennialists believe that Christ will not come until the thousand years have ended. Premillennialists believe that the world will grow worse and worse; post-millennialists believe that it will grow better and better. Between these two views there is no room for compromise, there can be no concession. One must be right and the other must be wrong. And let me again remind you, that this is in no sense a question of reason. It is not a question of what may seem to accord with our ideas or desires; it is not what may accord with our views, not what may seem reasonable, or appear likely. It is entirely and only and wholly a question of revelation. Let us beware of speaking of what God is or is not likely to do. For it is written, "My thoughts are not your thoughts, neither are your ways my ways, saith the Lord" (Isa. 4:8).

On the other hand, we cannot demand that all difficulties shall be removed, all questions answered, or all doubts solved, while no objection can be, or should be entertained if it be founded on human reason. For man's word is worthless when it is wholly a question of, What saith the Lord?

If God has said that the Millennium is to come first, then it will surely come. If God has said that the preaching of the Gospel is to convert the world, then no matter what the apparent difficulties may be, or what man may say about increase of population, insufficiency of means, and so forth, the world will surely be so converted. There is no lack of power with God, and if He has said it, He will most assuredly do it.

But if on the other hand, God has said that the object of the Gospel is to take out from the nations a people for His name, then no more can be done, let people preach, and persuade, and toil as they may. In either case, exactly what God has said will be done, no more and no less.

What then does the Word of God teach? Our subject as announced tells you our belief, that the premillennial advent of Christ is the truth of the Bible.

There are several ways of procedure by which this truth may be established, and many are the Scriptures which might be quoted. But as our time is limited it may accomplish a double object if we confine ourselves to those Scriptures which are usually referred to as supporting the postmillennial view.

Of course, the Scriptures may be perverted and wrested; they may be taken apart from their context; they may be interpreted so that when God says one thing, people may say He means another. All this can be done. The atheist may quote "there is no God," and the Devil may quote, or misquote, so as to serve his purpose. The only way to arrive at the mind of God is to study and believe it all, and take the text with the context. The Jews of old fell into error, yea the disciples failed to understand the Scripture, simply because they did not believe all Scripture. Jesus said to them:

> O fools, and slow of heart to believe all that the prophets have spoken: ought not Christ to have suffered these things, and to enter into his glory? (Luke 24:25–27).

They were slow to believe all. They did not want Christ to suffer, just as Christians now do not want Him to reign on earth. Christians like to dwell on the sufferings, and the Jews liked to dwell on the glory. But both alike come under the Savior's censure, "O fools, and slow of heart to believe all that the prophets have spoken."

Now let us look at a few Scriptures of the prophets and believe all.

1. Isaiah 11:9, "The earth shall be full of the knowledge of the LORD, as the waters cover the sea."

But note how this scene of blessedness is ushered in with judgment and Christ's coming in verse 4: "With righteousness shall he judge the poor, and reprove with equity for the meek of the earth: and he shall smite the earth with the rod of his mouth, and with the breath of his lips shall he slay the wicked" (that is, at the coming of Christ, see 2 Thess. 2:8).

2. Isaiah 2:2–3, "And it shall come to pass in the last days, that the mountain of the LORD's house shall be established in the top of the mountains . . . and all nations shall

flow unto it. And many people shall go and say, Come ye, and let us go up to the mountain of the LORD, to the house of the God of Jacob; and he will teach us of his ways, and we will walk in his paths."

Now note the context in which this prophecy occurs. The words immediately preceding declare that it is "concerning Judah and Jerusalem," and the words that immediately follow tell us that this shall be when "he shall judge among the nations, and shall rebuke many people: and they shall beat their swords into plowshares, and their spears into pruning hooks; nation shall not lift up sword against nation, neither shall they learn war any more." Thus we learn that this time of universal peace is ushered in by judgment, and not by the increase of Gospel light.

3. Isaiah 25:6–7, "And in this mountain shall the LORD of hosts make unto all people a feast of fat things, a feast of wines on the lees, of fat things full of marrow, of wines on the lees well refined. And he will destroy in this mountain the face of the covering cast over all people, and the vail that is spread over all nations."

From the preceding context (24:23) we learn that this mountain is Mount Zion on which "the LORD of hosts shall reign . . . before his ancients gloriously."

And from the context immediately succeeding (vv. 9–10, 12): "It shall be said in that day, Lo this is our God; we have waited for him, and he will save us: this is the LORD; we have waited for him, we will be glad and rejoice in his salvation. For in this mountain shall the hand of the LORD rest, and Moab shall be trodden down under him, even as straw is trodden down for the dunghill. . . . And the fortress of the high fort of thy walls shall he bring down, lay low, and bring to the ground, even to the dust." So that the spreading of the feast (which is no feast of gospel fat things), and this removing of the vail of error, will not take place until Christ, the One waited for, shall come.

4. Isaiah 35:1–2, "The wilderness and the solitary place shall be glad for them; and the desert shall rejoice, and blossom as the rose. . . . they shall see the glory of the LORD, and the excellency of our God."

But notice how this time of blessing and fruitfulness is introduced in verse 4:

"Say to them that are of a fearful heart, Be strong, fear not: behold your God will come with vengeance, even God with a recompense; he will come and save you. Then [not before] the eyes of the blind shall be opened," and all the scenes of millennial glory be revealed.

5. Isaiah 40:5, "And the glory of the LORD shall be revealed, and all flesh shall see it together: for the mouth of the LORD hath spoken it."

But read on and note verse 10: "Behold, the Lord GOD will come with strong hand, and his arm shall rule for him: behold his reward is with him, and his work before him."

6. Isaiah 66:10–14, "Rejoice ye with Jerusalem, and be glad with her, all ye that love her: rejoice for joy with her, all ye that mourn for her. . . . For thus saith the LORD, Behold, I will extend peace to her like a river, and the glory of the Gentiles like a flowing stream. . . . As one whom his mother comforteth, so will I comfort you. . . . And when ye see this, your heart shall rejoice."

Now note the next two verses (vv. 15–16): "For, behold, the LORD will come with fire, and with his chariots like a whirlwind, to render his anger with fury, and his rebuke with flames of fire. For by fire and by his sword will the LORD plead with all flesh: and the slain of the LORD shall be many." This does not look like gradual improvement and progress, resulting and ending in blessing and peace!

7. Psalm 2:8 is another verse that one hears constantly quoted on the platforms of missionary meetings, "Ask of me, and I shall give thee the heathen for thine inheritance, and the uttermost parts of the earth for thy possession."

But we never hear the next words of verse 9 quoted in connection with verse 8, yet there they stand: "Thou shalt break them with a rod of iron; thou shalt dash them in pieces like a potter's vessel"! But if the heathen are to be given to Christ by the preaching of the Gospel as the result of missionary effort, why are these converted nations to be broken and dashed in pieces in judgment? Even if it be said that the language is figurative, a rod of iron can surely be no figure of a message of peace; nor can a dashing in pieces be a figure of the Gospel of grace!

8. Zechariah 12:10, "I will pour upon the house of David, and upon the inhabitants of Jerusalem, the Spirit of grace and of supplications."

When? The verse before tells us "in that day, that I will seek to destroy all the nations that come against Jerusalem," and the same verse tells us that it shall be when "they shall look upon me whom they have pierced." Not therefore by the spread of Gospel light but by the seeing of the pierced One coming in judgment.

9. Zechariah 14:9, "And the LORD shall be king over all the earth: in that day shall there be one LORD, and his name one."

What day? Verse 1 tells us "The day of the LORD," when (v. 3) "then shall the LORD go forth, and fight. . . . And his feet shall stand in that day upon the mount of Olives." And so the succeeding context goes on to speak of "the plague wherewith the LORD will smite all the people that have fought against Jerusalem" (v. 12). This is what shall usher in that reign of peace.

Turn now to Daniel 7 and there you will find three verses often wrested from their context.

10. Daniel 7:14, "And there was given him dominion, and glory, and a kingdom, that all people, nations, and languages, should serve him: his dominion is an everlasting dominion, which shall not pass away, and his kingdom that which shall not be destroyed." Is this universal dominion given to Christ in connection with the spread of the Gospel? No, but at His coming.

Look at the preceding verse (v. 13): "I saw in the night visions, and, behold, one like the Son of man came with the clouds of heaven." Then "there was given him" not peace and righteousness but, "dominion and glory . . . that all . . . nations . . . should serve him."

11. Daniel 7:22, "The time came that the saints possessed the kingdom."

When did the time come? When "the Ancient of days

came"! And does He come at the conclusion of a Millennium of peace? No! The previous verse says: "I beheld, and the same horn made war with the saints, and prevailed against them; until the Ancient of days came, and [then, not until then] judgment was given to the saints of the most High; and the time came that the saints possessed the kingdom." It is clear therefore that Christ must come before there can be an end of war and the kingdom be possessed.

12. Daniel 7:27, "And the kingdom and dominion, and the greatness of the kingdom under the whole heaven, shall be given to the people of the saints of the most High." When? The verses immediately preceding tell us of a power that "shall speak great words against the most High, and shall wear out the saints of the most High. . . . But the judgment shall sit, and they shall take away his dominion, to consume and to destroy it unto the end" (vv. 25–26). Then follows the statement of verse 27.

It is in fact impossible to produce a Scripture which speaks of millennial blessing where the immediate context does not connect it with preceding judgment, or with the coming of the Lord Jesus Christ. In every instance the bright picture of rest and glory for the Jew, the Gentile, and the church of God, rests on the dark background of tribulation and judgment.

The New Testament is full of predictions of increasing and abounding evil; side by side with these there are "exceeding great and precious promises" for the poor and afflicted, the suffering and the sorrowful, the hated and persecuted, and this during the continuance of the present dispensation. There is no period between the present time and the coming of Christ in glory in which the saints are viewed or contemplated as being free from conflict; no time when they shall cease to "mourn" for the absent Bridegroom (Matt. 9:15), or be free from sorrow and tribulation (John 16:22–23), or have no need of "enduring to the end" (Matt. 10:22), or be other than "as sheep in the midst of wolves" (Matt. 10:16), no period when the wolves shall all become sheep, or the tares become wheat! And yet there is to come a blessed time when "there shall be no more curse." But that is essentially a divine work requiring all the might of omnipotence. Not to any body of men however holy or educated, not to any church however orthodox is committed the miraculous work of eradicating the curse from creation and sin from the heart. No! The church herself is fallible, erring, scattered, and divided, and needs herself to be brought to, and kept humbly at, the feet of the Savior.

But time will not permit us to go through all the Scriptures that refer to this subject. We can only remind you of certain great classes of passages:

1. the class that speaks directly of the object of the Gospel, "to take out of the nations a people for his name" Acts 15:14–17, Matthew 24:14, John 1:17, and so forth;

2. the class that describes the suffering condition of the church as "a little flock," and utterly precludes all idea of her increase and absorption of a converted world: Matthew 5:10–11, 44; 7:13–22; 9:15; Luke 18:8; John 15:18–21; 16:33; 17:14–16; Acts 14:22; 20:29–30; Romans 8:17–24; Philippians 3:18–21; 1 Thessalonians 5:1–8; 2 Timothy 2:12; Hebrews 10:30–37; 1 Peter 4:12–18;

3. the class that speaks of the condition of the world immediately before our Lord's return, comparing those days to the days before the flood: Matthew 24:37–39; Luke 17:26–30; 2 Peter 3:3–4, 2 Thessalonians 2:3–12; 1 Timothy 4:1–3; 2 Timothy 3:1–13; 2 Timothy 4:3–4; 2 Peter 2; Jude 17–18, and so forth;

4. another class that consists of warnings for the saints in view of increasing iniquity: "This know," 2 Timothy 3; "I charge Thee," 2 Timothy 4:1; "The Spirit speaketh expressly," 1 Timothy 4:1; "I stir up your pure minds by way of remembrance," 2 Peter 3:1.

Dear friends, the Scriptures everywhere speak of a coming conflict with ripened evil. It will be fierce but it will be decisive; the victory will be not by human power or might but by the power of Him who in His time shall show who is the blessed and only Potentate, King of Kings, and Lord of Lords. And they who take heed to the sure word of prophecy in their hearts will in that day cry out, "Lo! this is our God, we have waited for Him."

The coming of Him for whom we wait will not be the sunset of the world's bright day, but the dawning of the Sun of Righteousness at the end of the world's dark night. It is now night in this dark place, but the same Scripture that tells us it is night tells us also that it is "far spent," and that it will grow darker and darker until the end, and when the night is done, then the morning will come, the morning of millennial glory, that morning without clouds.

There is first the gloom and then the glory; first the darkness, then the dawn; first the conflict, and then the conquest.

Dear friends, that night is increasing, that gloom is thickening, that darkness is deepening. Oh, that this thought of the judgments that are impending, the great and terrible day of the Lord that is near, may make this a solemn truth and a great power and reality with us; that it may make prayer more earnest, souls more precious, and Christ more dear to our hearts. Oh, that the Lord may use and own this testimony by writing these things on our hearts; that some looking back from that glory might say of this service—it was there—it was on that day—that my heart was touched, that my eyes were opened, that my soul was delivered from darkness to light, and from the power of Satan to God.

CHAPTER 4

NO MILLENNIUM WITHOUT CHRIST

Immediately after the tribulation of those days shall the sun be darkened, and the moon shall not give her light, and the stars shall fall from heaven, and the powers of the heavens shall be shaken: and then shall appear the sign of the Son of man in heaven: and then shall all the tribes of the earth mourn, and they shall see the Son of man coming in the clouds of heaven with power and great glory (Matt. 24:29–30).

No consideration of the word of prophecy can be satisfactory which does not give full weight and importance to the last great prophetic utterance of the great prophet Himself. Let us approach it as worthy of and as commanding our deepest attention and closest consideration. We have not before us the visionary utterances of a mere enthusiast or the deceptive imaginations of a mere human, but the solemn prophetic announcement of "God manifest in the flesh."

Notice, first of all, that we have three records of two great prophecies: one recorded in Luke 21, and the other in Matthew 24 and Mark 23. These two statements appear to have been made on different occasions, in different places, and under different circumstances, and therefore naturally there is also a difference as to their subject matter.

In point of time, that recorded in Luke 21 appears to have been spoken first, and in the temple itself. Luke 21:5, "And as some spake of the temple . . . he said." It was "on one of those days, as he taught the people in the temple" (20:1), probably on the Tuesday, and before He left the temple with His disciples.

But that recorded in Matthew 24 and Mark 13 was uttered, "As he sat upon the mount of Olives over against the temple." Peter, James, John, and Andrew came to Him and asked Him certain questions privately. Here, the words of Jesus are the answer to definite questions. "When shall these things be? and what shall be the sign of thy coming, and of the end of the world [*consummation of the age,* RV mg]?" The Lord therefore tells them, and us, in this second prophecy . . . of the events which shall immediately precede and be the sign of His coming.

Now the first three or four verses of both discourses, and of all the three records are almost identical: Matthew 24:4–8; Mark 13:5–7; Luke 21:8–11. But here a remarkable change occurs that gives us the key to the right understanding of these prophecies. In Matthew and Mark the Lord goes on to speak of the sorrows of which those verses were "the beginning" and continues, and develops what He had begun to describe. But in St. Luke he stops short here; He does not go forward, but *goes back* to tell us what shall be "before all these things," and for thirteen verses (Luke 21:12–24) He speaks of what shall be before the beginning of sorrows, and to speak of the then impending destruction of Jerusalem, concluding at verse 24 with the words, "and Jerusalem shall be trodden down of the Gentiles until the times of the Gentiles be fulfilled." It is the concluding days of these "times of the Gentiles" that in Matthew and Mark the Lord enlarges on and describes the events that lead up to His appearing (Matt. 24:8–28, and Mark 13:9–23). Then all three records again coincide, and culminate in the grand and final "sign" about which the disciples had inquired.

To attempt to harmonize these prophecies without noticing the great diverging point of Luke 21:12 is to attempt the impossible; the best proof that it is so is the fact

that no commentator who treats all three records as referring to one and the same subject, succeeds in satisfying his
own mind, still less the minds of his readers.

But observing these notes of time, and this key to the
change of subject in Luke 21:12, we learn that in Matthew
24 and Mark 13 Jesus does not refer to the destruction of
Jerusalem at all. He begins long after that event, and gives
an epitome of the closing in of the last days of the "times of
the Gentiles," the days immediately preceding His coming
in glory with all His saints. In Luke 21, He devotes only
four verses to those events (vv. 8–11), and at verse 12 goes
back to tell us what shall be "before all these things."

In fact, these two discourses, taken together, are occupied
with three great subjects:

1. the destruction of Jerusalem,
2. the coming of Christ in glory, and
3. the events immediately preceding that coming.

In Matthew and Mark, Jesus enlarges on the events that
shall immediately lead up to His coming in glory. He fore-
tells the four great characteristics of the beginning of these
last events: wars (the red horse of the second seal, Rev. 6:4),
pestilences (the black horse of the third seal, Rev. 6:5–6),
famines (the pale horse of the fourth seal, Rev. 6:7–8), and
earthquakes (the sixth seal, Rev. 6:12). He speaks of the wit-
nessing Gospel (Rev. 6:2), and refers to a great event foretold by Daniel as a sure sign of the approaching end. The
tribulation then rapidly deepens until it reaches its cul-
minating point, and then, "Immediately after the tribulation
of those days . . . they shall see the Son of man coming in
the clouds of heaven" (Matt. 24:29–30).

Now in Luke, as I have said, there is little or nothing
about these awful and final events. In Luke 21:8–9, the
Lord refers to them, but pointedly says "the end is not
by and by [RV, *the end is not immediately*]." Then in
verses 10 and 11, He bears us rapidly forward to the end,
and almost anticipates verse 25. Thus, having thrust the
whole of those closing events into these four verses, the
Lord suddenly turns back, saying (v. 12) "But, before all
these things," and enlarges on the nearer, and then

impending woe of the city of Jerusalem. And when He says in verse 24, "Jerusalem shall be trodden down of the Gentiles, until the times of the Gentiles be fulfilled," the events that shall be the fulfilling of these very times form the chief subject of the discourse in Matthew 24 and Mark 13, which refers to that future siege.[1]

Thus of these two prophecies, part has been already literally fulfilled (Luke 21:12–24); and part remains to be also as literally fulfilled.

The great fact, however, that stands out most prominently in these prophecies, the evidence of which is absolutely overwhelming, is this: that our Lord leaves no room for any millennium of happiness and peace before He comes.

There is no controversy as to the literal fulfillment of Luke 21:12–24, for Jerusalem was literally "compassed by armies" (v. 20); the stones of its temple and walls were literally thrown down, though some of them were sixty feet long, by eight feet high, and ten feet broad; and Jerusalem is literally "trodden down of the Gentiles" (v. 24). But language is utterly useless if the word *until* does not mean that a time shall come when Jerusalem shall be no more trodden down, and when those times shall have an end! And we are all agreed that those times have not yet come to an end! We all know what mighty efforts have been made to end them, what wars have been waged, what crusades have been undertaken to end these times. But all in vain. Jerusalem is still trodden down of the Gentiles. No power has been able to end the period of Gentile supremacy. But when God's time has come to end it, no power on earth, nor all the powers combined, shall be able to prolong those times by a single day!

Now, let us remember that in Matthew and Mark, the Lord takes up the prophecy just when these "times of the Gentiles" are about to close with the last of Daniel's seventy *hebdomads*. Jesus enlarges on the determined desolations (see Dan. 9:26–27), and describes a time of future trouble to which the former cannot be compared. He says (Matt. 24:29), "Immediately after the tribulation of those days," and (Mark 13:24), "In those days, after that tribulation," and (Luke 21:24–25), when the "times of the Gentiles be fulfilled. And there shall be signs in the sun, and in the moon, and in the stars; and upon the earth distress of nations, with perplexity; the sea and the waves roaring; men's hearts failing them for fear, and for looking after those things which are coming on the earth: for the powers of heaven shall be shaken. And then shall they see the Son of man coming in a cloud with power and great glory." Truly there is nothing here that looks like a Millennium! The Lord leaves no room for it between the Tribulation and His personal appearing. The Tribulation ends with His coming. "Immediately," He says! Surely if He wished us to look for a Millennium of glory without Him, and before He comes, here was the time to mention it, here was the place to speak of it. But not only does He not do so, but He does the very opposite. Instead of describing His coming as following upon a period of peace and glory among the nations, He puts it "Immediately after the tribulation of those days," and as succeeding "distress of nations, with perplexity."

Those who think that in Matthew and Mark the Savior refers to the destruction of Jerusalem are compelled to interpret Matthew 24:30 of Titus and his armies: "They shall see the Son of man coming in the clouds of heaven with power and great glory." They call this "prophetic language," as though prophetic language were a totally different language from all other language. And so it must be if the coming of Titus was indeed the "lightning" of Matthew 24:27, which "cometh out of the east and shineth even unto the west"! But surely this very interpretation condemns itself and the whole system that is built upon it! For if verse 30, "then shall they see the Son of man coming in the clouds of heaven with power and great glory," means the coming of Titus with his armies, then in Matthew 26:64, Jesus must have meant the same when He said to His judges, "Hereafter shall ye see the Son of man sitting on the right hand of power, and coming in the clouds of heaven." And He must have spoken blasphemy and been guilty of death, because He made Himself equal to Titus! Such treatment of

Scripture stands self-condemned; it leaves no room at all for any future advent of Christ, in a prophecy which was an express answer to the question, "What shall be the sign of thy coming?"

Again, Jesus said (Luke 21:28), "Lift up your heads for your redemption draweth nigh." But in what way was the coming of Titus a ground for such a lifting up of the head, or for such a looking for redemption?

And note further that this lifting up of their heads is caused by no spread of Gospel light and peace among the nations. On the contrary, there is the greatest "distress of nations, with perplexity," "and then"—the very next thing is—(v. 27) "then shall they see the Son of man coming in a cloud with power and great glory."

Even when Jesus does speak about preaching the Gospel, He particularly informs us that it is only "for a witness to all nations" (Matt. 24:14, Mark 13:10), and not for the conversion of all nations.

And when He speaks of the setting up of "the abomination of desolation" (Matt. 24:15, and Mark 13:14), He refers to the prophet Daniel. But it is clear from Daniel 12 that this must be still future, for speaking of that same time of trouble the interpreting angel says to Daniel (12:1), "At that time shall Michael stand up, the great prince which standeth for the children of thy people: and there shall be a time of trouble, such as never was since there was a nation even to that same time: and at that time thy people shall be delivered."

Well, at the time when Titus came, Daniel's people were destroyed, and if that can be interpreted to mean "delivered" then language may mean anything and nothing, and there is an end of the whole matter!

There is one point, however, that does present an apparent difficulty in Matthew 24:34, Mark 13:30, and Luke 21:32, "Verily I say unto you, This generation shall not pass, until all these things be fulfilled." It is quite true that the word *generation* is used not merely of a period of so many years, but it means, even as in English, "a race," or "a stock," especially in its moral character. "God is in the

generation of the righteous" (Ps. 14:5); "This is the generation of them that seek him" (Ps. 24:6); "The generation of
the upright shall be blessed" (Ps. 112:2); "The children of
this world are in their generation wiser than the children of
light" (Luke 16:8); "Ye are a chosen generation" (1 Peter
2:9). The moral character of the generation of the rejecters
of Jesus shall be maintained to the end, for corporate bodies continue to exist, notwithstanding the passing away of
their individual members.

But while all this is true, it is also true that the pronoun
this is demonstrative, and I would ask, may it not refer to
the generation then in the speaker's prophetic vision? Jesus
is speaking very emphatically of the actual beginning of
these final events that immediately precede His coming,
and He is addressing those who see the beginning of these
things: "And when these things begin to come to pass, lift
up your heads" (Luke 21:28); "When ye shall see these
things come (RV *coming*) to pass" (Mark 13:29). The Great
Prophet is standing amid those future scenes. He speaks to
whoever may witness the beginning, or the "becoming" of
the Tribulation. He says that the generation that sees the
beginning will see the end. All will be comprised in that
one generation. The period between the beginning of the
Tribulation and the end of the age will be very brief, and
the same generation that sees the one will witness the other.

There arises therefore here a very natural question that
we may well ask, and it is this: Is there any sign by which
we may know this beginning of the Tribulation and thus lift
up our heads? Yes. The Savior anticipates our question, and
in Matthew 24:32, Mark 13:28, and Luke 21:29, He gives
the parable of the fig tree. "Behold the fig tree, and all the
trees; when they now shoot forth, ye see and know of your
own selves that summer is now nigh at hand. So likewise
ye, when ye see these things come to pass, know ye that the
kingdom of God is nigh at hand" (Luke 21:29–31), "even at
the doors"! (Matt. 24:33; Mark 13:29). The sign of the coming is similar to the sign of summer (Blessed summer for
the saints of God, for it tells of deliverance from the winter
of the Tribulation. It tells of their "escape" from those

things which are coming on the earth, and of standing before the Son of Man, Luke 21:36).

We may know with certainty that the season is near, though we can predicate nothing as to the day. We may know with certainty that when the tribulation of the last days begins, it is the beginning of the end and the redemption of the waiting church is so near that the Lord Himself has already commenced His descent to gather His saints to Himself, and meet them in the air. Before the breaking of a single "seal" (Rev. 6) He will have called to His saints, "Come up hither" (Rev. 4:1), and they shall be safely housed with Him amid the scenes of heavenly worship (Rev. 4 and 5). Hence His word of encouragement: "When these things begin to come to pass, then, look up and lift up your heads for your redemption draweth nigh" (Luke 21:28). The beginning of these awful scenes is the moment of the church's deliverance.[2]

It must always be a matter of uncertainty as to which of the world's great trials is the beginning of the last. Therefore no one can know. "Of that day and hour knoweth no man, no, not the angels of heaven, but my Father only" (Matt. 24:36). But it will be "as in the days of Noah" (v. 37), when no one is expecting it, that His saints shall be separated. "They knew not until the flood came and took them all away; so shall also the coming of the Son of man be. Then shall two be in the field, the one shall be taken and the other left. . . . Watch ye therefore; for ye know not what hour your Lord doth come" (Matt. 24:37–42).

Here we have a distinct reference to 1 Thessalonians 4:16–17, when at the very beginning of the Tribulation "the Lord himself shall descend from heaven with a shout, with the voice of the archangel and with the trump of God; and the dead in Christ shall rise first: then we which are alive and remain shall be caught up together with them in the clouds, to meet the Lord in the air: and so shall we ever be with the Lord." And so shall we "stand before the Son of man," "accounted worthy," in all His worthiness, "to "escape these things" that shall then come on the earth (Luke 21:36).

The beginning of the Tribulation marks the time when

the Lord will thus come for His saints, and the height and end of it marks the time when He will appear in glory with all His saints.

Surely it behooves us to heed the warning with which the Lord concludes His great prophecy in Luke 21:34–36:

> Take heed to yourselves, lest at any time your hearts be over-charged with surfeiting, and drunkenness, and cares of this life, and so that day come upon you unawares. For as a snare shall it come on all them that dwell on the face of the whole earth.[3] Watch ye therefore, and pray always, that ye may be accounted worthy to escape all those things that shall come to pass, and to stand before the Son of man.

Christians who are looking for a Millennium without Christ are, it is evident from Christ's last great prophecy, greatly deceived. Christians who are looking for the improvement of the world will see it in the increasing "distress of nations." Christians who are looking for the progress of the church will see it in the progression of the downgrade of error, departure from the faith, and corruption of truth!

How much more blessed in the obedience of faith to be "looking for the blessed hope, and appearing of the glory of our great God and Savior Jesus Christ, who gave himself for us." It is one thing to escape the Tribulation, it is another thing to go through it.

Dear friends, amid the scenes which shall soon issue in the beginning of that Tribulation, may we heed this warning and escape it by being now separated from the world by Christ, found in Him, and gathered to Himself at His coming; washed from our sins, sheltered from wrath, safe from judgment through the precious blood of that same Jesus.

Endnotes

1. The word "immediately" marks off the prophecy in Matthew from that recorded in Luke, where we have instead long "times of the Gentiles" following on the siege of Jerusalem.

2. For a fuller answer to this question see the appendix, which shows that the time seems to be near when God will deal once again with His ancient people and that we are already near the beginning of the end!
3. It is obvious that this can in no sense apply to Titus and his armies coming against Jerusalem.

CHAPTER 5

THE CALLING AND HOPE OF THE CHURCH OF GOD

*Unto me, who am less than the least of all saints, is this
grace given, that I should preach among the Gentiles the
unsearchable riches of Christ; and to make all men see what
is the fellowship of the mystery, which from the beginning
of the world hath been hid in God (Eph. 3:8–9).*

F ew words are used in as many different senses as the
word *church*, and therefore it behooves us to be careful
as to our employment of it. For example:

1. It is used of a particular church, as the Church of
Rome, Jerusalem, Antioch, or the Church of England.

2. It is often wrongly used of the ministry, and people
speak of this as "entering the church."

3. It is used of a separate assembly meeting for worship in
any given building or room, as the Church of England
defines it (in the *Nineteenth Article of Religion*), "a congregation of faithful men, in which the pure Word of God
is preached, and the sacraments be duly administered."

4. It is used of the building in which such a congregation
meets for worship.

5. It is used of the Church Episcopal, as distinguished
from the non-Episcopal (Chapel).

6. It is used of the great body of nominal Christians, bad and good alike, tares and wheat, professors and possessors.

7. It is used of "the blessed company of all faithful people." I need hardly say that this last is the sense in which it is viewed in this chapter, and in which we are now to consider it.

Now this Ephesians passage contains a somewhat difficult construction. The apostle concludes chapter 2 by showing how Jew and Gentile are one body in Christ (2:16), and are "builded together for an habitation of God through the Spirit" (2:22). Then chapter 3 begins, "For this cause I Paul, the prisoner of Christ for you Gentiles." Then follows a long parenthesis, beginning with verse 2 and not ending until the end of verse 13. He then takes up the thread at verse 14 by repeating the expression of verse 1, "For this cause I bow my knees unto the Father of our Lord Jesus Christ, of whom the whole family[1] in heaven and earth is named."

"For this cause," because Jew and Gentile are one body in Christ. "I bow my knees," in prayer for "the whole family."

Now this parenthesis, Ephesians 3:2–13, flows naturally from the proposition of chapter 2. These Ephesian saints had been idolators of the Gentiles, and the apostle has shown how they had been quickened and built together in Christ. As the instrument in the hands of the Spirit the apostle had been used to preach the Gospel to them, and in doing this he had suffered and for their sakes was now a prisoner of Jesus Christ. Then, before continuing his subject and praying for the strengthening and growth of that body (3:16–21), he breaks off, and in this parenthesis he stops to dwell on the grace shown to the Gentiles. In our text he calls it "the unsearchable riches of Christ."

Now these words are generally separated from their context and taken in some undefined sense to express the resources treasured up for us in Christ.

The fact, of course, is true, and we rightly sing:

> How vast the treasure we possess
> In thee O Lord, our Righteousness;
> All things are ours in Christ, Thy Son,
> With whom Thy love hath made us one.

While this as a fact is blessedly true, the question is, Is this the mind of the Spirit here? I think not.

There are riches in Christ which we may call the *searchable* riches, such as the revealed prophecies and promises concerning Him, which could be searched and understood by the prophets who wrote them. But there were others which they could not search. They were "unsearchable."

The Greek word here rendered "unsearchable" occurs twice, here, and in Romans 11:33), and each time it is translated differently. It means, "that which cannot be traced or tracked, untrackable." Here it is rendered "unsearchable," and in Romans 11:33 "past finding out." There is another word translated "unsearchable" in Romans 11:33, but that denotes that which cannot be understood even if found, "inscrutable." "O the depth of the riches both of the wisdom and knowledge of God! how [inscrutable] are His judgments and His ways [untrackable (RV *past tracing out*)]." So here in our text the word does not mean that which cannot be understood if found, but that which cannot be traced or followed out.

These untrackable riches of Christ which the prophets could not trace out, are not merely the blessing of the Gentiles as such, as might be inferred from Ephesians 3:6. That was never any secret. It was revealed from the beginning to Abraham that "in thee shall all families of the earth be blessed" (Gen. 12:3); "All the nations of the earth shall be blessed in him [Abraham]" (Gen. 18:18). Many prophecies reveal this truth of which aged Simeon testified when he spoke of Christ as "a light to lighten the Gentiles, and the glory of thy people Israel" (Luke 2:32).

These untrackable riches of Christ, therefore, were not merely the blessing of Gentiles, as such, by and by, but the taking out of a people from among them now (Acts 15:14)

to form the one body in Christ, the mystery of the church.
This is what had, until now, been hidden, and what had
now been specially revealed to Paul. In testimony of this,
note the following Scriptures:

> Now to him that is of power to stablish you according to my gospel,
> and the preaching of Jesus Christ, according to the revelation of the
> mystery,[2] which was kept secret since the world began, but now is
> made manifest, and by the scriptures of the prophets,[3] according to
> the commandment of the everlasting God made known to all
> nations for the obedience of faith (Rom. 16:25–26).

Speaking of Christ's body:

> The church [the apostle says]: whereof I am made a minister, accord-
> ing to the dispensation of God which is given to me for you, to ful-
> fill the word of God; even the mystery which hath been hid from
> ages and from generations, but now is made manifest to his
> saints: to whom God would make known what is the riches of the
> glory of this mystery among the Gentiles; which is Christ in you [mg
> *Christ among you*, that is, among you Gentiles as well as among the
> Jews], the hope of glory: whom we preach (Col. 1:24–27).

> Ye have heard of the dispensation of the grace of God which is
> given me to you-ward: how that by revelation he made
> known unto me the mystery; (as I wrote afore in few words,
> whereby, when ye read, ye may understand my knowledge in
> the mystery of Christ) which in other ages was not made known
> unto the sons of men, as it is now revealed unto his holy apos-
> tles and prophets by the Spirit: that the Gentiles should be fel-
> lowheirs, and of the same body, and partakers of his promise in
> Christ by the gospel: whereof I was made a minister, according
> to the gift of the grace of God given unto me by the effectual
> working of his power. Unto me, who am less than the least of
> all saints, is this grace given, that I should preach among the
> Gentiles the unsearchable riches of Christ; and to make all men
> see what is the fellowship of the mystery, which from the
> beginning of the world hath been hid in God, who created all
> things by Jesus Christ: to the intent that now unto the princi-

palities and powers in heavenly places might be known by [RV, *by means of*] the church the manifold wisdom of God, according to the eternal purpose (RV mg *the purpose of the ages*) which he purposed in Christ Jesus our Lord (Eph. 3:2–11).

Now the Old Testament prophets knew nothing of all this. They looked, as it has been said, from the one hilltop of Christ's sufferings to the other hilltop of His glory, but the valley that lay between was unknown. They could not track it, and all its mines of wealth were unexplored. The Spirit, by Peter, refers to this when he says:

Of which salvation the prophets have enquired and searched diligently, who prophesied of the grace that should come unto you: searching what, or what manner of time the Spirit of Christ which was in them did signify, when it testified beforehand the sufferings of Christ, and the glory that should follow. Unto whom it was revealed, that not unto themselves, but unto us they did minister the things, which are now reported unto you by them that have preached the Gospel unto you with the Holy Ghost sent down from heaven; which things the angels desire to look into (1 Peter 1:10–12).

But when Christ had been rejected, when atonement had been made, then the message of reconciliation could be sent forth. Then, and not until then, was that which had been hid in God and kept secret from the beginning of the world made known. Then the eternal purpose of God was revealed, and the riches of the valley (this present interval between the sufferings and the glory) were laid bare, that pilgrims and strangers who now are passing through it may trace and search them out.

And who are these pilgrims and strangers? They are those who once were dead in trespasses and sins (Eph. 2:1), but who have been "quickened together with Christ" (2:5), saved by grace (2:8), and made fellow-heirs with Christ (3:6), "members of his body, of his flesh, and of his bones" (5:30–32). This is the great mystery concerning Christ and His church.

Notice how Ephesians 5:31 is quoted from Genesis

2:24, where the words are spoken of the first Adam; and how true they are of Christ, the second man, the last Adam. While He (as the world thinks) sleeps in death, while He is absent in the heavenlies, the Lord God takes from His pierced side an Eve, all living, to be His bride! And when she fell in the first Eve, He, like the first Adam, "was not deceived" (1 Tim. 2:14), but unlike the first Adam He did not charge His bride with the transgression! No! He charged Himself with it. He followed her to the depths of her fall, and knowing all the consequences, He took her sins upon Himself, bore all the judgment of God's wrath due to her sins, and cleared her from every spot and every stain.

> Christ also loved the church and gave himself for it . . . that he might present it to himself a glorious church, not having spot, or wrinkle, or any such thing; but that it should be holy and without blemish (Eph. 5:25, 27).

Oh, what love! How wondrous in itself, but how blessed to know the truth of all this in our own selves, each one, individually, before God. How blessed to know that the heavy debt has been paid, not only when we had nothing to pay, but before we even knew that we had contracted the debt! This is good news, dear friends. This is the Gospel, the glorious Gospel of the grace of God. This is the burden of the angelic definition of the Gospel in Luke 2:11, as revealed in the divine titles, a Savior, Christ, the Lord—a "Savior," not a helper, a Savior for the lost, not a helper of those who can help themselves; "Christ," that is, God's anointed Savior, the Savior whom God had anointed, provided, given, and sent, not some savior we have made for ourselves; and then, the "Lord," the Lord of all power and might, able to save to the uttermost all that come to God by Him. Yes, this is the good news, that God has anointed a Savior, not a helper, who is able to save. The will of God is the source of it all (Heb. 10:7). The work of Christ is the channel of it (v. 10), and the witness of it in our hearts is the Holy Spirit of God (v. 15). This is the work of the Holy Spirit in the world now.

In Genesis 24 we have a beautiful illustration of the Holy

Spirit's work in the mission of Eliezer to seek a bride for the only and beloved son of his master. Like Eliezer He comes to us now with the tokens of the Father's wealth, and the pledges of the Son's great love, "the earnest of the Spirit" (Heb. 10:22). He seeks out the predestined bride; He espouses her to one husband, that He may present her as a chaste virgin to Christ (see 2 Cor. 11:2); He takes of the things of Christ and reveals them to her (John 16:14–15); He shows her "things to come" (John 16:13); He teaches her and guides her to all truth (John 14:26; 16:13). By nature she was buried in idolatry, and now she is led out and led on, as a pilgrim and a stranger through this world, to meet her Beloved. What attraction has the world for her as she journeys on to meet her Lord? This meeting and union with Him is the very object for which she was called and for which she lives. And as she approaches the end of her journey and as her long day[4] draws to its close—presently—"at the eventide" (Gen. 24:63) her Isaac will come forth to meet her and receive her to Himself and present her to Himself in glory. Her Bridegroom has now gone to prepare a place for her (John 14:1–3), and meanwhile he "cleaves" to her and supports her (Gen. 2:24). Oh, how much higher than our poor thoughts are His ways! Our thoughts do not rise higher than trying to cleave to Him: man represents her as some poor drowning one trying to cleave to a rock! No, dear friends, this is not the truth! It is not the weaker one trying to cleave to the stronger one, but it is the strong one cleaving to the weak one, as it is written: "Therefore shall a man leave his father and his mother and shall cleave unto his wife, and they shall be one flesh" (Gen. 2:24). "This is a great mystery but I speak concerning Christ and the church" (Eph. 5:32). Yes! and He will cleave to His poor bride until He perfects in glory what He has begun in grace, until caught up to meet Him in the air, she shall be forever with the Lord.

This is the calling of the church, and this is her hope. She has turned from idols to her beloved Lord. She tries to serve Him, "the living and true God," while she "waits for His Son from heaven" (1 Thess. 1:9–10). This is the work of the Holy Spirit in this the dispensation of the Spirit, "To make ready a people prepared for the Lord" (Luke 1:17); to "save some" (2 Cor. 9:22); to "take out of the nations a people for his name" (Acts 15:14); and "a remnant from Israel according to the election of grace" (Rom. 11:5); baptizing them all into "one body," bestowing on them "one calling," and giving them all "one hope" (Eph. 4:4–6).

Now we are waiting for the fruition of this hope and looking for His appearing. Having been betrothed to Him we long for the marriage day to come. The scene of that marriage is to be in the glory. It is called "the marriage of the Lamb" (not of the bride), for His is the greater joy, in glory as well as in grace.[5]

It is His pleasure, His honor, and His glory to do all this for poor vile sinners. And when He shall have assayed their service (2 Cor. 5:10; 1 Cor. 3:12–15), and awarded their crowns (2 Tim. 4:7–8), heaven shall ring with the marriage song, while yet the bride is with Him in the heavenlies, before the heaven opens (Rev. 19:11), and she appears with Him in glory. The words of the marriage song are given: "Alleluia: for the Lord God omnipotent reigneth. Let us be glad and rejoice, and give honor to him: for the marriage of the Lamb is come, and his wife hath made herself ready" (Rev. 19:6–7).

So long as the Bridegroom tarries and is absent, the bride mourns and fasts, even as He foretold. "The days will come, when the bridegroom shall be taken from them, and then shall they fast" (Matt. 9:15; see Mark 2:19–20; 2 Sam. 19:24). But at His coming His own words shall be fulfilled: "And the glory which thou gavest me I have given them" (John 17:22). Ah, then indeed, there shall be joy in heaven, joy to the Lamb, joy to His bride, joy to all that are called to partake of this wondrous scene. But in all things He must have the pre-eminence, and great as must be the joy and gladness of the bride in Him, His joy in her must be the greater. This is "the joy that was set before him," for which He "endured the cross, despising the shame" (Heb. 12:2). That He might teach us all this, and set it all before us, marriage was His first institution in Eden, a marriage was the occasion of His first miracle where He turned the water into wine, and "manifested forth his glory." He limits the day of grace with this aspect of the day of glory when He said, "I will drink no more of this fruit of the vine, until I drink it new with you in the kingdom of God" (Matt. 26:29).

His last message to His bride is, "Surely I come quickly" (Rev. 22:20), and she cries through her tear-dimmed eyes, "Even so, come Lord Jesus." Each night as she lies down to sleep she prays that He may come before the morning, and each morning as she rises, she prays that He may come before the night, for her Lord has told her thus to watch. She is to regard each day as it comes as *the* day, for what she does not know is whether He will come "at even, or at midnight, or at the cock-crowing, or in the morning" (Mark 13:35). Hence she listens with opened ears for the longed for summons, "Come up hither," and waits to enter the door that shall then be opened in heaven (Rev. 4:1).

Dear friends, will you be there? These words of grace and glory are not merely words to preach about, they are wondrous realities, and solemn too, for this day of grace will not last forever. We know not how soon it may end. But we do know this, that your last day will dawn, your last hour will strike, the last warning will be given, the last sermon will be heard, the last prayer will be offered, and then, unless you are found in Christ and are clothed with His righteousness, you must be forever lost.

Would you escape that doom? Then listen to Him who "spake as never man spake," and said, "all that the Father giveth me shall come to me, and whoso cometh unto me I will in no wise cast out."

Dear friends, may you prove the truth, and know the blessedness of this promise and the importance of this precept, "let your loins be girded about and your lights burning . . . blessed are those servants whom the Lord when he cometh shall find watching."

Genesis 14

Thine the beauty and the glory—
Heir of all things—Son of God,
Shining round me and before me,
Lighting all the desert road.

Camels girded for the journey—
Kneeling, laden, set for home:
Ah, my heart is gone already,
Centred there, no more to roam.

Roll afar, thou proud Euphrates!
Nought can keep me from my bourne,
Where my mighty Guardian came from—
There with me will He return.

Buried in Chaldea's city,
I had perished with my race;
But the Steward came to save me,
Met me in his Master's grace.

Asked me for "a little water"—
Let me quench his camels' thirst,
Saw in me, Bethuel's daughter,
Her he prayed for at the first.

Ah, the errand that he told me,
Of the "Living One" who died—
Of the Father's love and counsel,
Taking unto Him a bride!

Nothing, I remember nothing,
But that sacrifice and choice—
Never music filled my spirit
Like that penetrating voice.

Could I hear Him, "Eliezer,"
And for Isaac not be won?

Ah, the Father loved and sought me—
Sent and claimed me for his Son.

Let the token on my forehead,
Let the bracelet on my hand,
Prove me now the chosen daughter
Of the Lord of all the land.

I will go; I would not tarry;
Object of that heart's delight!
He was unto death obedient;
I would walk with him in white.

Jewels, raiment, gifts, the servant
Brought for me from Isaac's hand:
Precious things, that else had never
Shone in any foreign land.

I shall see Him in His beauty—
He, Himself, His bride will meet;
I shall be with Him forever—
In companionship complete.

Thoughts of Him are strength and gladness
What man comes there forth our way?
"'Tis my Master!" 'tis the Bridegroom:
Veiled—the bride is caught away.

And the servant telleth Isaac
All the things that he had done:
And Rebekah reigns in Hebron—
Wife of the once offered One.

Endnotes

1. It cannot be "every family" as in the RV: (1) simply because it is not true, for Ephesians 4:6 declares that there is only "one body," one family of the saved in Jesus Christ; the families of the ungodly, the children of the Devil, are certainly not the subjects of this blessing

and honor that is peculiarly and distinctly the possession of the family of the redeemed; and (2) because the
exactly corresponding structure of the Greek in other
passages is not so translated by the revisers themselves,
for example: Romans 1:29 and John 5:17; 1:9, "all
unrighteousness," not "every"; Matthew 23:35, "all the
righteous blood," not "every": "all Jerusalem"; Acts
7:22, "all the wisdom."

2. The Greek word means, not that which cannot be
   understood, but a secret revealed or communicated to
   one initiated.
3. The New Testament prophets referred to in Ephesians
   4:11, "And he gave some apostles, and some prophets."
   See also 1 Corinthians 12:28; Ephesians 2:20; Acts
   11:27; 13:1; 15:32; Romans 12:6.
4. 1 Thessalonians 5:5–8.
5. In Luke 15, it is the Father's joy to save, the Spirit's to
   seek, and the Son's to find, and the joy is not the joy of
   the angels, as is generally erroneously represented, but
   it is joy *"in the presence of* the angels of God."

CHAPTER 6

THE CHURCH'S MOTIVE FOR SERVICE

Beloved, now are we the sons of God, and it doth not yet appear what we shall be; but we know that, when he shall appear, we shall be like him; for we shall see him as he is. And every man that hath this hope in him purifieth himself, even as he is pure (1 John 3:2–3).

Every one that hath this hope purifies himself, and only such as have it. For this hope is the peculiar possession of the sons of God, who know something of what manner of love the Father hath bestowed upon them.

Then, observe, that this hope, though it is the blessed possession of the sons of God, is not centered in themselves, but it is fixed upon another. The words "in him" mean, literally, "upon him," that is, upon Christ. Hence the RV translates it, "Every one that hath this hope set on Him." It is not who hopes, for that would refer to the act of hoping, whereas he who has this hope has it as a permanent possession, fixed on Christ as the glorious object. Then, its action is ever present; it purifies. When we see Him, we shall be like Him, therefore if we want to be like Him now, we must behold Him and be occupied with Him. He is pure. Purity belongs to Him, and our purity is secured by occupation with Him in the glory. "We, beholding, are changed into the same image from glory to glory." Here is no restless effort, no anxious toiling. It is simply we beholding, beholding, are changed. Here is the divine prescription for conformity to the image of Christ; here is that which will transfigure us and make us like Him.

Now our text lays down this great principle that the coming of Christ in glory is not a mere doctrine to be preached, not a mere theory to be held, not a mere dogma to be believed, but it is the mighty motive for all true Christian service. It is a hope that is bound up inseparably with all doctrines, all ordinances, all precepts, and all practice.

For example, we desire to walk worthy of the vocation wherewith we are called. We desire to walk worthy of the Lord unto all pleasing, to be fruitful in every good work, diligent in all service. Then the question is, How shall we accomplish this? What must we do in order to attain this desired end?

Man, of course (even the spiritual man), is ready with his various rules for holy living, for he is by nature a Pharisee, and is always ready to do something. Even when he confesses that he has been "justified by grace" he would like to be sanctified by works! He forgets that God has "made Him [Jesus] to be unto us, justification and sanctification," and that we are not justified in Christ by grace without an effort, and then left to be sanctified in ourselves by our own effort.

Truly, in this—in the highest things as well as in the lowest—in this, as in all beside, God's thoughts are not human thoughts, nor His ways our ways (Isa. 4:8). Man says that faith is that which will produce holiness of living; God says it is hope. Man says it is faith in Christ's power to keep me—if I can only keep my own faith! But God says it is hope in Christ's coming for me that will purify me, and this blessed hope He has given me as my permanent possession.

At the very best, all this is only a human substitute for God's divine prescription. It shuts out the true way and gives a false way; it shuts out the only efficacious means and presents powerless means; it shuts out the substance and gives a shadow.

God's way of making our walk correspond with our holy calling is to fill us with the blessed hope of Christ's coming and to occupy us with His glory, so that "we beholding . . . are changed." The human way is to occupy us with ourselves: with our spiritual lives, which are to be deepened; with our faith, which is to be increased; with our walk, which is to be perfected. God's way is to point us to Christ's glory in heaven; the human way is to point us to Christ's power in us. God says the hope of coming glory will purify us; man says it is the power of present faith that will do it.

Oh, dear friends, beware of any presentation of doctrine that takes your eye from Christ! Beware of any phase of it that puts anything however minute, however plausible, however apparently good, between your heart and Christ. Beware of building on the promises instead of on the Promiser; beware of being occupied with the blessing instead of with the Blesser. If the mere blessing be the object of our lives, we shall most certainly never attain it. But having the Blesser we have all He can give, and His richest blessing will be with us without an effort.

Hence, you will observe here that it is not the doctrine of Christ's second coming that will do anything for us, but it is Christ who is coming on whom this, our purifying hope, is set.

This necessarily keeps the heart in contact with Christ. This contact secures our abiding in Him without striving to abide. This abiding is the source of all fruitfulness and obedience (John 15:5). Hence the power of this hope. Even the Buddhists have a saying, If you think of Buddha and pray to Buddha you will become Buddha. So the one who looks and waits for God's Son from heaven will be like Enoch, the seventh from Adam. He will walk with God, for he knows that at any moment it may be said of him "he was not, for God took him." It is easy for superficial readers and thinkers to pronounce the apostles mistaken in looking for the Lord in their day. But no one can be mistaken who thus realizes the power and blessing of this purifying hope. The apostles and early Christians were no more mistaken than the saints who yesterday fell asleep. For their Christian characters were, alike, shapen and formed by having their hope set on Him. And happy shall we be if we are like them in thus looking for His appearing. Note now, some of the practical uses that the Holy Spirit makes of this blessed hope in the Word of God.

1. It is a powerful motive with the sinner to make him turn from his evil ways. The command to repent stands frequently connected with the Lord's coming (Matt. 3:2; Acts 3:19–20; 17:30–31). All the passages that speak of the nearness of the day of the Lord—its suddenness, its terrors for the ungodly—all appeal powerfully to the neglecter of the great salvation. If this doctrine be true, it is evident that it is not merely a question of the uncertainty of life (which is the point of most pulpit appeals), but of the certainty of Christ's coming. "When once the master of the house hath risen up, and hath shut to the door." All depends on this: the movement of Christ! While He is seated at God's right hand the door of mercy is open; when He is risen up, it will be shut! And yet preachers neglect this powerful motive and introduce another which the Scriptures do not urge.

2. Again, why is a man not profited if he "gain the whole world and lose his own soul?" (Matt. 16:26). Why? Because, the next verse tells us, "the Son of man shall come in the glory of his Father with his angels and then shall he reward every man according to his works." That is why. If someone could gain the whole world, it would be useless, for the Lord is coming to judge it.

3. Why is the case of mere professors, who say "Lord, Lord," so hopeless (Matt. 7:21)? Because, the next verse tells us, "in that day . . . then will I profess unto them, I never knew you, depart from me." That is why!

4. How does Jesus warn us not to be ashamed of Him and of His words now (Mark 8:38)? By reminding us in the next verse that "of him also shall the Son of man be ashamed when he cometh in the glory of his Father with the holy angels."

5. What is the true comfort for those who are troubled at Christ's absence? Not, you shall die and come to Me, but "I will come again, and receive you unto myself; that where I am, there ye may be also" (John 14:1–3).

6. What is true comfort in bereavement? "Comfort one another with these words." What words? Words that tell of the reunion of those who have fallen asleep with those who are alive and remain, when the Lord Himself shall descend from heaven to receive both into His presence. "So [lit., *thus, in this manner*] shall we ever be with the Lord" (1 Thess. 4:13–18). The Great Comforter Himself likewise connected true comfort with resurrection. "Thy brother shall rise again" (John 11:23). But man has improved on that and has quite a different mode of comforting bereaved ones now. He quite dispenses with the hope of the advent and of resurrection and bids all mourners to comfort themselves with a kind of Christian spiritualism that quiets everyone, good and bad alike, with the delusion of all going to heaven when they die!

7. The hope of a groaning creation is bound up with the manifestation of the saints with Christ in glory. "For the earnest expectation of the creature [*creation*, RV] waiteth for the manifestation of the sons of God . . . because the creature [*creation*, RV] itself also shall be delivered from the bondage of corruption, into the glorious liberty [RV, *into the liberty of the glory*] of the children of God" (Rom. 8:19–23).

8. With what motive are we urged not to judge one another now, and not to be moved when others judge us (1 Cor. 4:3–4)? The next verse says, "Therefore judge nothing before the time, until the Lord come, who both will bring to light the hidden things of darkness, and will make manifest the counsels of the hearts: and then shall every man have praise of God."

9. If we are exhorted to draw near with faith and take the bread and wine in memory of our Lord's death at His first advent, we cannot, or ought not to, do it without connecting it with His second advent (1 Cor. 11:26): "For as often as ye eat this bread and drink this cup, ye do show the Lord's death till he come."

10. Is love for the person of Christ set before us as the greatest and most important of all things? It is so, in consideration of the fact that He is coming again. "If any man love not the Lord Jesus Christ let him be anathema [accursed], Maranatha [our Lord cometh]" (1 Cor. 16:22). It is the fact of the Lord's coming that puts every thing in its right place. The apostle had much to complain of in this first epistle to the Corinthians. In chapter 1, divisions; chapter 4, false judgments; chapter 5, uncleanness; chapter 6, brother going to law with brother; chapters 10–11, errors in ritual; chapter 15:35, errors of doctrine; but when he comes to the last verse in that epistle, when it is a question of Maranatha, when things are weighed in the light of that all-pervading fact of the Lord's coming, then he does not say, if anyone be not moral or orthodox or whatever, but "if any man love not the Lord Jesus Christ," as much as to say—Nothing but love for Christ will stand us in any stead when our Lord comes. A person may be perfectly moral, orthodox, and correct in ritual, and yet have no love for Christ! This fact of the Master's coming puts all these things in their proper place, and tells us that the Lord alone shall be exalted in that day, and only those who have His love shed abroad in their hearts by the Holy Spirit shall be exalted with Him.

11. Are we exhorted to "grieve not the Holy Spirit of God" (Eph. 4:30)? It is added, "whereby ye are sealed unto the day of redemption."

12. Are we exhorted to "be sober"? The exhortation is based on the same motive (1 Thess. 5:2–6).

13. Are we exhorted to forbearance and gentleness? (for this is the meaning of the word in Phil. 4:5), "Let your moderation be known unto all men"? The reason for it is "the Lord is at hand," and He therefore will put all right that is now so wrong. And if His coming be so near, such things are not worth contending for.

14. Have we "need of patience, that," after we have done the will of God we "might receive the promise" (Heb. 10:36)? The motive for it is found in the next verse: "For yet

a little while, and he that shall come will come, and will not tarry." And again, "Be patient therefore, brethren, unto the coming of the Lord" (James 5:7).

15. Are we exhorted to mortify the flesh? This is still the mighty motive, "When Christ, who is our life, shall appear, then shall ye also appear with him in glory. Mortify therefore your members which are upon the earth" (Col. 3:4–5).

16. Does the apostle pray that his Philippian converts "may be sincere and without offense"? It is with reference to and "till the day of Christ" (Phil. 1:9–10).

17. If John exhorts his "little children" to "abide in him," the exhortation is pointed with this motive "that, when he shall appear, we may have confidence, and not be ashamed before him at his coming" (1 John 2:28).

18. If our faith be tried, it is that it "might be found unto praise and honor and glory at the appearing of Jesus Christ" (1 Peter 1:7).

19. We are bidden to "rejoice, inasmuch as ye are partakers of Christ's sufferings." Why? "that, when his glory shall be revealed, ye may be glad also with exceeding joy" (1 Peter 4:13).

20. If we are exhorted to "watch unto prayer," it is because "the end of all things is at hand" (1 Peter 4:7).

Here are twenty examples, and a hundred might easily be given. But these will be sufficient to show that the doctrine is no mere visionary enthusiasm, or fanaticism, but is one of the most practical of all the truths revealed in the Word of God.

But there is one aspect which we must consider at greater length, and that is its connection with missionary work.

There is nothing more urgently and frequently laid to its charge than that this doctrine tends to paralyze missionary effort. But the tree is known by its fruit, and, so far from this being the case, we find one among the primitive churches which is indeed a model church, the church of Thessalonica. It received abundant and almost unqualified praise, and it was emphatically a missionary church. The apostle writes:

Ye were ensamples to all that believe in Macedonia and Achaia.
For from you sounded out the word of the Lord not only in
Macedonia and Achaia, but also in every place your faith to
God-ward is spread abroad (1 Thess. 1:7–8).

And this church was all this because of the Christian
character of its members. That character was formed on all
truth, and hence it was not deformed. It was perfect in its
threefold completeness.

1. They had "*turned* to God from idols,
2. to *serve* the living and true God, and
3. to *wait* for God's Son from heaven" (1 Thess. 1:9–10).

Yes. They waited for God's Son from heaven. Not for
death, or providence, or Titus, or the world's conversion, or
the restoration of the Jews, or the reconstruction of the
Roman earth, but for God's Son from heaven. This one subject occupies one quarter of these two epistles to the
Thessalonians—one verse in four! a dozen passages in four
or five pages that speak of the coming of God's Son from
heaven! Every chapter contains a reference to it (1 Thess.
1:10; 2:17–20; 3:11–13; 4:13–18; 5:1–6, 13; 2 Thess.
1:6–10; 2:1–12; 3:5). No wonder it was a missionary
church! No wonder it was a model church!

Again, there are facts that none can gainsay. The early
Christians were characterized by two things, (1) their doctrine was intensely millenarian, and (2) their practice was
intensely missionary.

They waited and looked for the Lord, and they went
everywhere preaching the Word. And the period in the later
history of the church was marked by the absence of these
two things that generally go together. A man may have a
missionary spirit and yet not look for Christ's return. But it
is impossible for one who "waits for God's Son from heav-
en" not to do his utmost to "sound forth the word of the
Lord in every place."

Did not the Savior tell us that it was the wicked servant
who said in his heart, "My lord delayeth his coming"? Did
He not warn us of the three great dangers that flow from the
evil heart that cherishes such a thought?

1. Self-indulgence. He begins "to eat and drink with the drunken."

2. Self-assertion. He begins "to smite his fellow-servants."

3. Self-delusion. "The Lord of that servant shall come in a day when he looketh not for him, and in an hour that he is not aware of" (Matt. 24:48–50; Luke 12:45–46).

No! Our Lord's coming, when held in the power of the doctrine, is the greatest possible incitement to missionary work and to pastoral fidelity, integrity, and zeal.

Look at 1 Peter 5:2–4:

Feed the flock of God which is among you, taking the oversight thereof, not by constraint, but willingly; not for filthy lucre, but of a ready mind; neither as being lords over God's heritage, but being ensamples to the flock. And when the chief Shepherd shall appear, ye shall receive a crown of glory that fadeth not away.

And 2 Timothy 4:1–2 (RV):

I charge thee in the sight of God and of Christ Jesus, who shall judge the quick and the dead, and by His appearing and His kingdom: preach the word; be instant in season, out of season, reprove, rebuke, exhort with all long-suffering and teaching.

And Philippians 2:16:

Holding forth the word of life; that I may rejoice in the day of Christ, that I have not run in vain, neither labored in vain.

These are the appeals of Scripture as to ministerial and missionary work and zeal, and how powerful is the message carried under such motives! Look at the appeal to the heathen idolators (Acts 17:30–31), or to the scoffers and mockers (Jude 14–15). How powerful and weighty are these motives for and subjects of preaching. And the consolation for the workers, how sweet, based on the same blessed truth:

I have fought a good fight, I have finished my course, I have kept the faith: henceforth there is laid up for me a crown of righteousness, which the Lord, the righteous judge, shall give me at that day: and not to me only, but unto all them also that love his appearing (2 Tim. 4:7–8).

No, dear friends, there can be no paralyzing of missionary effort when its very key note is, "I must work while it is day for the night cometh when no man can work."

On the contrary, the doctrine of the Lord's speedy coming puts all work in its right place. It tells us that the great object of the preaching of the Gospel is not the conversion of the world, which would put off that coming to an indefinite day, or for a thousand years at least. The professing church has told the world that its mission is to convert it, but she deceives the world. The world can turn around and taunt her with her failure, while it can point to the awful fact that it is fast converting the professing church to its own worldliness.

It all depends, however, on what the Gospel was sent and meant to do. If the Gospel was meant to convert the world, it will be a failure if this is not done. But if the Gospel was meant "to take out . . . a people for his name," then it is not a failure, for this is being done. If it was sent that God might in mercy "save some," then it is not a failure. If it was given that a company that no one can number might be saved out of every people and kindred and nation, then it is no failure, for that is being done. If it was sent that it might be "preached for a witness unto all nations," then it is not a failure, for this is being done. And these are the objects of the Gospel, and therefore of missionary labor, "according to the Scriptures."

All the prophets and apostles agree in testifying that the world will never know blessing without the Blesser; will never know peace until the Prince of Peace shall come; and will never know righteousness "until he comes whose right it is," until "a king shall reign in righteousness."

The prophets and apostles of old were animated by no such false hopes. One said, "Lord, who hath believed our report" (1 John 12:38; Rom. 10:16). Another said, "The love of Christ constraineth us," not the hope of success. They strove as "stewards" to be faithful (1 Cor. 4:1–3), and looked for the commendation, "Well done good and faithful servant"—not good and successful. Yes, it is the love of Christ, the love of a crucified, risen, ascended, and returning Savior that alone will enable anyone to obey the last great command, Go! preach the gospel to every creature. There our commission begins and ends. We have nothing to do with results. As stewards we must be found faithful, and no apparent failure can dishearten us if we only bear in mind that "known unto God are all his works from the beginning of the world," and that His Word cannot return to Him void. It must prosper in the thing whereunto He has sent it, and His purpose and counsel must stand forever.

Thus, this mighty motive breathes its peace into the hearts of Christian workers, takes away all anxiety, and removes all fear. Need I contrast with this the powerlessness and inadequacy of any other or lower motives, which lead to the frantic efforts of too many in the present day, who believe the world is to be converted before Christ comes and that man can do it if he likes! No wonder that such are tempted to lose faith in the power of the simple Word of God and take up every new scheme, adopt every fresh novelty, and try every fresh panacea, aiming at reformation rather than at regeneration, hardly touching the fringe of the masses, and then leaving those whose characters they have improved and reformed just as far from the kingdom of heaven.

No, dear friends, "that which is born of the flesh is flesh, and that which is born of the Spirit is spirit. . . . Ye must be born again" (John 3:8–9). And the Gospel has lost none of its ancient power. It is, as much today as when it was first preached, "the power of God unto salvation." It needs no pity, no help, and no servant. It can overcome all obstacles and break down all barriers. No human device need be tried to prepare the sinner to receive it, for if God has sent it no power can hinder it; if He has not sent it, no power can make it effectual.

Dear friends, let us as Christian ministers and workers esteem it our highest privilege to be workers together with God in a work that cannot possibly fail. Let us receive into our hearts this mighty motive for holy living and effective service. Remember how it is used by the Holy Spirit in the Word as the ground of its appeals, the point of its arguments, and the basis of its exhortations; "knowing the time, that now it is high time to awake out of sleep: for now is our salvation nearer than when we believed. The night is far spent, the day is at hand: let us therefore cast off the works of darkness, and let us put on the armor of light" (Rom. 13:11–12).

CHAPTER 7

THE SECOND ADVENT IN RELATION TO THE JEW

For I would not, brethren, that ye should be ignorant of this mystery, lest ye should be wise in your own conceits; that blindness in part is happened to Israel, until the fullness of the Gentiles be come in. And so all Israel shall be saved: as it is written, there shall come out of Zion the Deliverer and shall turn away ungodliness from Jacob: for this is my covenant unto them, when I shall take away their sins. As concerning the gospel, they are enemies for your sakes: but as touching the election, they are beloved for the fathers' sakes. For the gifts and calling of God are without repentance (Rom. 11:25–29).

We have before us in these words a large and important subject, so large that volumes have been written upon it without exhausting it; so important that it forms the very fabric of this blessed Book.

It is impossible to do more than glance at its outlines in one brief address. But no consideration of the subject can be satisfactory that does not go back to the beginning and lay its foundations deep in the everlasting covenant referred to so pointedly in our text, "This is my covenant."

All God's dealings with Israel, past, present, and future,

spring from this covenant. All are based upon it. Israel is beloved for the fathers' sakes, for what God has given He does not take back; "the gifts and calling of God are without repentance [RV mg Gr. *not repented of*]." A preordained plan lies at the foundation of the history of Israel.

Immediately before Abram received these gifts and calling of God, in Genesis 11, God had divided the nations and had given them their inheritance in the earth, with special reference to Israel. We read in Deuteronomy 32:8–9:

> When the most High divided to the nations their inheritance, when he separated the sons of Adam, he set the bounds of the people according to the number of the children of Israel. For the LORD's portion is his people; Jacob is the lot of his inheritance.

The judgment of the Flood was unheeded by the nations, and the people soon gave themselves over to idolatry. Abram's family formed no exception as we learn from Joshua 24:2, where Joshua reminds the people of the fact, saying, "Your fathers dwelt on the other side of the flood in old time, even Terah, the father of Abraham, and the father of Nahor: and they served other gods." Well may the Spirit lay such stress on the grace that called Abraham and the promise that was freely given to him; for surely it was all of pure and free grace when the God of glory appeared to him, put his idols to confusion, and called him to Himself, saying, "I . . . have severed you from other people, that ye should be mine" (Lev. 20:26). The sevenfold promise in Genesis 12:2–3 tells us that when Abram was called, it was not merely from idolatry but to blessing. God was the performer of all things for him (Ps. 57:2).

1. I will make of thee a great nation.
2. I will bless thee.
3. I will make thy name great.
4. Thou shalt be a blessing.
5. I will bless them that bless thee.

6. I will curse him that curseth thee.
7. In thee shall all families of the earth be blessed.

You have the same form of sevenfold, or perfect blessing when God established His covenant in Exodus 6:4–8.

1. I will bring you out.
2. I will rid you of their bondage.
3. I will redeem you.
4. I will take you to me for a people.
5. I will be to you a God.
6. I will bring you in unto the land.
7. I will give it [the land] for an heritage.

And then it is solemnly signed, I, Jehovah!

But now let us look at the significant scene when this wondrous covenant was first made. It is most important and full of the deepest instruction.

We all know that a covenant is usually made between two parties, with certain conditions to be observed on each side. When both parties are human these conditions may or may not be kept, and when they are broken by either side the covenant is null and void.

Now, all such conditional covenants which man has ever made with God have been shamefully broken. Whenever he who is "conceived in sin and shapen in iniquity" has entered into covenant with the eternal and holy God, he has "turned aside like a broken bow," and the covenant has failed.

But there is such a thing as an unconditional covenant, which is really a free-grace promise, but formally made by the one contracting party. And when this one is Jehovah Himself, then it cannot fail, and it must stand forever— "ordered in all things and sure."

There are three such unconditional covenants in the Bible: one with Noah concerning the earth, in virtue of which we today enjoy "seed-time and harvest and cold and heat, and summer and winter, and day and night" and immunity from a flood of waters. This covenant is seven times mentioned in Genesis 9:8–17. The second is with Abraham concerning the land (Gen. 15:8–21). And the third is with David concerning the throne (2 Sam. 7:4–29; 23:5; Ps. 89).

The covenant that was made with Israel at Sinai was a conditional covenant. God covenanted to give them life and blessing, peace and prosperity in the land, and Israel covenanted to obey the Law.

> All the people answered . . . and said, All the words which the LORD hath said will we do. . . . And he [Moses] took the book of the covenant, and read in the audience of the people: and they said, All that the LORD hath said will we do, and be obedient. And Moses took the blood, and sprinkled it on the people, and said, Behold the blood of the covenant, which the LORD hath made with you concerning all these words (Ex. 24:3, 7–8; compare Heb. 9:18–20).

In contrast with all this, it is expressly recorded that when God reinstates Israel in the blessing it will be on the ground of grace and not of Law; on the ground of a "new" and unconditional covenant and not on the conditional covenant of Sinai.

> Behold, the days come, saith the Lord, that I will make a new covenant with the house of Israel, and with the house of Judah: not according to the covenant that I made with their fathers in the day that I took them by the hand to bring them out of the land of Egypt; which my covenant they brake! (Jer. 31:31–32).

Now let us turn to Genesis 15 and see how this original, unconditional, covenant was made by Jehovah with Abraham. Abraham was fully instructed how he was to proceed, and what preparations he was to make (vv. 9–10). He divided the heifer, the goat, and the ram, and "laid each piece one against the other," that when the time came he might pass between the pieces. For this was, or became, the manner of making a covenant, as we learn from Jeremiah 34:18–19, where Jehovah says:

> I will give the men that have transgressed my covenant, which have not performed the words of the covenant which they had

made before me, when they cut the calf in twain, and passed between the parts thereof, the princes of Judah, and the princes of Jerusalem, the eunuchs, and the priests, and all the people of the land, which passed between the parts of the calf.

But here, in this case, just at the critical moment when Abram was ready to pass between the parts of the victims and be a party to the covenant, God put him to sleep! for "when the sun was going down, a deep sleep fell upon Abram, and lo, an horror of great darkness fell upon him" (v. 12), and he saw "a smoking furnace and a burning lamp that passed between those pieces. In the same day the Lord made a covenant with Abram, saying, Unto thy seed have I given this land, from the river of Egypt unto the great river, the river Euphrates" (vv. 17–18). Here then we have the great unconditional covenant, made by only one contracting party, and that one the Lord God Himself.

In this fact we have the simple explanation of that difficult verse, Galatians 3:20, of which a university professor recently stated he had counted 430 interpretations! The apostle is speaking of two things, the covenant, or "promise" made with Abraham, and the covenant, or the "Law," made with Israel; he says (v. 17) that "the covenant, that was confirmed before of God in Christ, the law, which was four hundred thirty years after, cannot disannul, that it should make the promise of none effect." The Law was given, he says "in the hand of a mediator." That shows there were two contracting parties. But when there is only one covenanting party there is no mediator; when the covenant was made with Abram there was only one, and that one God! "Now a mediator is not a mediator of one, but God is one," that is, when He gave Abram the promise. Hence the covenant was unconditional and cannot be disannulled by a conditional covenant made 430 years after by Israel with God. "Wherefore then serveth the law? It was added because of transgressions, till the seed should come to whom the promise was made" (v. 19). For the covenant ran "unto thy seed" (Gen. 15:8) "which is Christ" (Gal. 3:16).

We all know, however, that Abraham never possessed the land. Then this covenant was ratified in Isaac, "unto thee, and unto thy seed" (Gen. 26:3), but he possessed it not! for "Isaac gave up the ghost and died . . . and Jacob buried him" (Gen. 35:29). And then it was ratified in Jacob, "to thee will I give it, and to thy seed" (Gen. 28:13), but he possessed it not, for "Jacob dwelt in the land wherein his father was a stranger" (Gen. 37:1), he died in Egypt (49:33), and all that he possessed in the land was *a burying place!*

Nevertheless, the covenant is sure. All blessing is based upon it, and referred to it. When God heard the groaning of Israel in Egypt, it was because "God remembered His covenant" (Ex. 2:24). When He came down to deliver them, we read, "I have established my covenant with them" (Ex. 6:4). When He would comfort them, He says, "He will not . . . forget the covenant of thy fathers which he sware unto them" (Deut. 4:31). When, again and again, He had compassion on them in their rebellion and foolishness, we read, "He remembered his holy promise, and Abraham his servant" (Ps. 105:42). "They remembered not. . . . They soon forgat. . . . They forgat God their savior. . . . Nevertheless he regarded their affliction, when He heard their cry: and he remembered for them his covenant" (Ps. 106:7, 13, 21, 44–45). Hence David sings, "He will ever be mindful of his covenant" (Ps. 111:5), and Jehovah declares, "My covenant will I not break, nor alter the thing that is gone out of my lips" (Ps. 89:34).

But besides this covenant with Abram to give him the land, there was that other covenant (also unconditional) that was made with David concerning the throne (2 Sam. 7), which is also to be confirmed and fulfilled only in David's seed. The promises of this covenant are referred to in the expression "the sure mercies of David,"[1] sure because they rest on God's faithfulness and holiness. See Psalm 89:28, "My mercy will I keep for him forevermore, my covenant shall stand fast with him," and verse 35, "Once have I sworn by my holiness that I will not lie unto David." It is interesting to note that both these unconditional covenants are linked with the first to Noah, in one Scripture.

Thus saith the Lord; If ye can break my covenant of the day, and my covenant of the night, and that there should not be day and night in their season; then may also my covenant be broken with David my servant. . . . Then will I cast away the seed of Jacob, and David my servant, so that I will not take any of his seed to be rulers over the seed of Abraham, Isaac, and Jacob: for I will cause their captivity to return, and have mercy on them (Jer. 33:20–21, 26).

It is on the strength of this everlasting covenant made to Abraham, Isaac, and Jacob that Jesus based His proof of the resurrection. For if the blessing and glory in the land was made to the individual patriarch as well as to the nation, saying "to thee and to thy seed" in the case of each patriarch, then there must be a resurrection. The patriarchs never had any possession in the land except a sepulcher, for which they paid the Canaanites. Hence when the question about resurrection was put to Jesus, He refers to this very fact which depends on, and arises out of, the covenant. The Lord's answer to the Sadducees is generally interpreted as referring to a condition of things that renders a resurrection unnecessary and makes the whole argument meaningless. Notice the words. Matthew 22:31, "But as touching the resurrection of the dead, have ye not read"; Mark 12:26, "And as touching the dead that they rise, have ye not read"; Luke 20:37, "Now that the dead are raised, even Moses showed at the bush, when he calleth the Lord the God of Abraham, . . . Isaac, . . . and Jacob." The whole point is concerning resurrection, and the argument is contained in the fact that as this unconditional covenant was made with the patriarchs and cannot be broken, so likewise it cannot be fulfilled unless they rise from the dead.

We are all aware, however, of the present sad and scattered condition of the nation of Israel. But all their sufferings—without a country, without a king, without the knowledge of saving truth—all is the consequence of their own conditional covenant at Sinai.

God gave them a law, holy, just, and good. He gave it to prove to them their own impotence and to lead them to the omnipotence of the Savior He had provided.

The prophets spoke of His glory, but they also predicted His rejection. He became the hope of those who believed in Him; the consolation of Israel to those who waited for Him; and redemption to those who looked for Him.

At length He came to His own inheritance, as the seed of Abraham; to His own throne, as the seed of David, but His own people received Him not (John 1:11). He was despised, rejected, and crucified. This is the heir, they said. Yes, the heir of the land and the heir of the crown! But they said, let us kill Him, and in ignorance they did it. They "knew Him not" (Acts 13:27). "They knew not what they did" (Luke 23:34). And yet they were guilty, for though they did it in ignorance as to His person, they did it not in innocence as to His blood. They had full proof of Jesus' innocence. One of the malefactors said, "This man hath done nothing amiss" (Luke 23:41). His judge said, "I find no fault in him" (Luke 23:4). Pilate's wife said, "that just man" (Matt. 27:19); the heathen soldier when he saw Him expire, said, "This was a righteous man" (Luke 23:47); when he saw the signs that followed, he cried out, "Truly this man was the Son of God" (Mark 15:39). In spite of all this testimony they bribed false witnesses and put Him to death.

They did not "believe all that the prophets had spoken" (Luke 24:25), and thus a portion of truth separated from the rest blinded them to their ruin. But according to the typical illustration in 2 Kings 11, the king has been rescued from among the slain; He is hid in the heavenly temple above. The king has "sat down" because His redemption work is done, but He is "expecting" because the years have not yet run their course. Here comes in the "mystery" of the church. Like Jehosheba her "life is hid with Christ in God" (2 Kings 11:2; Col. 3:3), like Jehoiada she goes out in testimony for the king whom all else think to be dead. She can have no sympathy, part, or lot, with Athaliah the usurper. Here and there some are let into the secret of the covenant and the oath (2 Kings 11:4) and many a loyal heart beats for the rejected king, and longs for the day of His manifestation.

But meantime the usurper holds the rule, and Jerusalem

is trodden down of the Gentiles until the times of the Gentiles be fulfilled. There can be no hope for Jerusalem and no hope for Israel except as based on the everlasting covenant. And the claims of the Heir can be met only in and by Christ's coming again in virtue of that covenant, to receive "the throne of his father David," and to "reign over the house of Jacob forever" (Luke 1:32–33). Here is the secret of all future blessing for Israel.

All this was foreshown in Psalm 89:30–37. Speaking of David it was written:

> If his children forsake my law, and walk not in my judgments; if they break my statutes, and keep not my commandments; then will I visit their transgression with the rod, and their iniquity with stripes. Nevertheless my lovingkindness will I not utterly take from him, nor suffer my faithfulness to fail. My covenant will I not break, nor alter the thing that is gone out of my lips. Once have I sworn by my holiness that I will not lie unto David. His seed shall endure for ever, and his throne as the sun before me. It shall be established forever as the moon, and as a faithful witness in heaven. Selah.

Part of this has literally come to pass. David's children did forsake God's law. Their transgression has been visited with the rod and their iniquity with stripes. Then the rest of this prophecy shall also literally be fulfilled, and God will not break His covenant, though Israel broke His statutes.

> The children of Israel shall abide many days without a king, and without a prince, and without a sacrifice . . . afterward shall the children of Israel return, and seek the LORD their God, and David their king; and shall fear the LORD and his goodness in the latter days" (Hos. 3:4–5).

In Amos 9 we have another powerful description of this.

> For, lo, I will command, and I will sift the house of Israel among all nations, like as corn is sifted in a sieve, yet shall not the least grain fall upon the earth (v. 9).

Why? For what purpose are they preserved? See verse 14–15:

> And I will bring again the captivity of my people of Israel, and they shall build the waste cities, and inhabit them; and they shall plant vineyards, and drink the wine thereof; they shall also make gardens, and eat the fruit of them. And I will plant them upon their land, and they shall no more be pulled up out of their land which I have given them, saith the LORD.

But before they can rejoice in the blessings of the glorious and peaceful reign of "David their king," the Lord Jesus Christ, they will experience the tribulation under the Antichrist. This is spoken of in many of the prophets, but at greater length in Daniel and Revelation. It appears from many prophecies that the nation is not to be gathered all at once, or all at one and the same time. The first thing that transpires is that before the appearing of Christ in glory and before the great ingathering of Israel, which will then take place, a smaller and partial and informal assembling, such as we see, it may be, the beginnings of at the present moment, will take place. We read Zechariah 14:2–4:

> I will gather all nations against Jerusalem to battle; and the city shall be taken, and the houses rifled. . . . Then shall the LORD go forth, and fight against those nations, as when he fought in the day of battle. And his feet shall stand in that day upon the mount of Olives.

Thus, it is against Israel that this battle shall be waged, and it is in connection with this battle that the Lord comes. When He thus comes, Israel, in part at least, are already in Jerusalem. The tribes of Judah and Levi are mentioned by name in Zechariah 12, where the same events are spoken of.

> Behold, I will make Jerusalem a cup of trembling unto all the people round about, when they shall be in the siege both against Judah and against Jerusalem. And in that day will I make Jerusalem a burdensome stone for all people (Zech. 12:2–3).

Joel also speaks of the same siege.

For, behold, in those days, and in that time, when I shall bring again the captivity of Judah and Jerusalem, I will also gather all nations, and will bring them down into the valley of Jehoshaphat (Joel 3:1–2).

Ezekiel describes the land as at this time partially and sparsely inhabited. Speaking to the Antichrist Jehovah says,

And thou shalt say, I will go up to the land of unwalled villages; I will go to them that are at rest, that dwell safely, all of them dwelling without walls, and having neither bars nor gates, to take a spoil, and to take a prey; to turn thine hand upon the desolate places that are now inhabited, and upon the people that are gathered out of the nations, which have gotten cattle and goods, that dwell in the midst of the land. . . . And thou shalt come up against my people of Israel, as a cloud to cover the land; it shall be in the latter days, and I will bring thee against my land, that the heathen may know me, when I shall be sanctified in thee, O Gog, before their eyes (Ezek. 38:11–12, 16).

From Zechariah 12:9–10, so it is also clear that repentance is then bestowed upon Israel by the true Joseph who then makes himself known to his brethren.

And it shall come to pass in that day, that I will seek to destroy all the nations that come against Jerusalem. And I will pour upon the house of David, and upon the inhabitants of Jerusalem, the spirit of grace and of supplications: and they shall look upon me whom they have pierced, and they shall mourn for him, as one mourneth for his only son.

From Matthew 24:55 and 2 Thessalonians 2:4 it also appears that the temple will be, in some measure at least, rebuilt; for "the abomination of desolation"[2] spoken of by Daniel the prophet in connection with this time of "Jacob's trouble," when his (Daniel's) people shall be delivered, is seen, set up and standing in the holy place (Dan. 12:11, RV).

This preliminary and partial gathering, if we may so speak of it, seems designed for the great purpose of chastisement (Jer. 30:7–9), ending in Israel's repentance and conversion.

> Thus saith the Lord GOD; Because ye are all become dross, behold, therefore I will gather you into the midst of Jerusalem. As they gather silver, and brass, and iron, and lead, and tin, into the midst of the furnace, to blow the fire upon it, to melt it; so will I gather you in mine anger, and in my fury, and I will leave you there, and melt you. Yea, I will gather you, and blow upon you in the fire of my wrath, and ye shall be melted in the midst thereof. As silver is melted in the midst of the furnace, so shall ye be melted in the midst thereof; and ye shall know that I the LORD have poured out my fury upon you (Ezek. 22:19–22).

Zechariah also speaks of this "elect remnant" when God says,

> And I will bring the third part through the fire, and will refine them as silver is refined, and will try them as gold is tried: they shall call on my name, and I will hear them: I will say, It is my people: and they shall say, The LORD is my God (13:9).

This elect remnant[3] is doubtless the 144,000 of Revelation 7, sealed and preserved through the Great Tribulation, thus refined and purified.

Thus while this first installment of the restoration of Israel is in anger and judgment; there is another stage—a larger and final gathering spoken of, after the Lord has appeared in glory. Isaiah 11 seems to clearly point to this when he calls it the "second": "And it shall come to pass in that day." What day? The day when, according to verse 4, He has destroyed Antichrist with the breath of His lips and the glory of His coming (2 Thess. 2:8).

> And it shall come to pass in that day, that the Lord shall set his hand again *the second time* to recover the remnant of his people, which shall be left, from Assyria, and from Egypt, and from Pathros, and from Cush, and from Elam, and from Shinar, and

from Hamath, and from the islands of the sea. And he shall set up an ensign for the nations, and shall assemble the outcasts of Israel, and gather together the dispersed of Judah from the four corners of the earth. . . . And the LORD shall utterly destroy the tongue of the Egyptian sea; and with his mighty wind shall he shake his hand over the river, and shall smite it in the seven streams, and make men go over dry shod. And there shall be an highway for the remnant of his people, which shall be left, from Assyria; like as it was to Israel in the day that he came up out of the land of Egypt (Isa. 11:11–12, 15–16, italics mine).

And they shall bring all your brethren for an offering unto the LORD out of all nations upon horses, and in chariots, and in litters, (mg *coaches*), and upon mules, and upon swift beasts, to my holy mountain Jerusalem, saith the LORD (Isa. 66:20).

When shall this gathering be? After the judgment and war already referred to, for verses 15–16, say:

Behold, the LORD will come with fire, and with his chariots like a whirlwind, to render his anger with fury, and his rebuke with flames of fire. For by fire and by his sword will the LORD plead with all flesh: and the slain of the LORD shall be many.

And then, after verse 19 shall have been fulfilled, where the LORD says: "and I will send those that escape of them unto the nations, to Tarshish, Pul, and Lud, that draw the bow, to Tubal, and Javan, to the isles afar off, that have not heard my fame, neither have seen . . . my glory among the Gentiles." We then come to the gathering described in verse 20.

The means employed in this gathering will be partly instrumental, as we learn from this Scripture (Isa. 66:19–20), and from others, such as Isaiah 49:22–23,

Thus saith the Lord GOD, Behold I will lift up mine hand to the Gentiles, and set up my standard to the people: and they shall bring thy sons in their arms, and thy daughters shall be carried upon their shoulders. And kings shall be thy nursing fathers, and their queens thy nursing mothers.

But we have just seen that the means shall be also miraculous; God's own act (Isa. 11:15–16). It is in this respect that this second part of the ingathering differs from the first, of which nothing is said about the means beyond ordinary natural causes such as we now see going on around us.

Further, we learn from Ezekiel that when the nation is thus fully gathered, it will be in an unconverted state.

> For I will take you from among the heathen, and gather you out of all countries, and will bring you into your own land. *Then* will I sprinkle clean water upon you, and ye shall be clean: from all your filthiness, and from all your idols, will I cleanse you (Ezek. 35:24–25, italics mine).

Jeremiah likewise shows that this conversion and cleansing will follow immediately upon this restoration (Jer. 31:27–34).

And now only a few references which speak

1. of the physical blessings which will be experienced by the land, blessings which can never be produced by any increase of holiness in the church, but only by the miraculous acts of God Himself: Isaiah 11:6–9; 25:1–2, 6; 55:13; Amos 9:13;

2. of the spiritual blessings which will be enjoyed by the people: Hosea 1:10; Jeremiah 30:31; 23:6; and

3. of the millennial blessing experienced by the whole earth: Micah 4:8; Isa. 2:1–3; 27:6; 60:20–22; 62:3; 65:12; Jeremiah 3:17; Psalms. 45:16–17; 72.

When we think of these circles of blessing, may we not ask with the apostle, "Now if the fall of them be the riches of the world, and the diminishing (mg *decay or loss*) of them, the riches of the Gentiles, how much more their fullness? For if the casting away of them be the reconciling of the world, what shall the receiving of them be, but life from the dead?" (Rom. 11:15).

If the twelve apostles and one hundred and twenty disciples have sent the message of reconciliation to the uttermost parts of the earth, what will not all Israel do when saved and filled with this fullness of blessing and power from on high?

The Spirit's answer is that it will be like "life from the dead," nothing less than like a resurrection for Israel, the world, and the creation! The analogy is most wonderful, the comparison is divine; it is given and revealed to us by Him who alone knows what it will be.

Dear friends, when we think of God's wondrous purposes concerning Israel and the blessing that is bound up in Israel for the whole world, well may we pray for the peace of Jerusalem. Well may we heed the words of the prophet:

> For Zion's sake will I not hold my peace, and for Jerusalem's sake I will not rest, until the righteousness thereof go forth as brightness, and the salvation thereof as a lamp that burneth. . . . Ye that make mention of the LORD, keep not silence, and give him no rest, till He establish, and till he make Jerusalem a praise in the earth (Isa. 62:1, 6–7).

Well might David end the Seventy-second Psalm, which sets forth the glory, when in Israel all the nations of the earth shall be blessed, "Blessed be the LORD God, the God of Israel, who only doeth wondrous things, and blessed be His glorious name for ever: and let the whole earth be filled with his glory; Amen, and Amen." And well might he add, "The prayers of David the son of Jesse are ended," for when the whole earth shall be filled with His glory, prayer will indeed be turned to praise!

Endnotes

1. Isaiah 55:3; Acts 13:34.
2. *Abomination* is a common term for an idol (1 Kings 11:5–7; 2 Kings 23:13). In the RV, Daniel 9:27 reads, "Upon the wing of abominations shall come one that maketh desolate," that is, upborne by demoniacal power shall the Antichrist come. With this agrees 2 Thessalonians 2:9; Revelation 13:2, 13–15.
3. We must distinguish between this "elect remnant"

(Joel 2:32, and others), saved through and out of the
Tribulation; and the "Elect nation" (Isa. 65:9, 22, and
others), which is all Israel as chosen out of, and distinguished from all other nations; and "the remnant
according to the election of grace" (Rom. 11:5), which
is the company of Israelites saved now by grace, and
made members of Christ's body, the church.

CHAPTER 8

THE SECOND ADVENT IN RELATION TO THE GENTILE

And in the days of these kings shall the God of heaven set up a kingdom, which shall never be destroyed: and the kingdom shall not be left to other people, but it shall break in pieces and consume all these kingdoms, and it shall stand for ever. Forasmuch as thou sawest that the stone was cut out of the mountain without hands, and that it brake in pieces the iron, the brass, the clay, the silver, and the gold; the great God hath made known to the king what shall come to pass hereafter (mg, "after this"): and the dream is certain, and the interpretation thereof sure (Dan. 2:44–45).

One of our duties toward the Word of God is to rightly divide it, because it is the word of truth. And because it is the engrafted word we are to receive it; because it is the faithful word we are to hold it fast; because it is the word of Life we are to hold it forth. But because it is the word of truth we are to rightly divide it. It is one of the verities of that word that "what God hath joined together, let no man put asunder" (Matt. 19:6), and so we may assert as truth the corollary of this proposition and say what God has put asunder, let no one join together; what God has separated and distinguished, let no one confound and confuse.

Now if God has put anything asunder, He has done so in 1 Corinthians 10:32, where He has forever distinguished "the Jew, the Gentile, and the church of God." But man has not rightly divided the Word of God with reference to these three; he has joined them together with all perverseness and self-will, giving to the church what God has said is for Israel, and to the world what God has said is for the church. In the prophecies, man puts the church for Israel when it is a question of *blessing,* while he carefully leaves all the curses for the Jew. So in practical religion he confuses the church with the world so completely that one cannot tell the difference between the worldly church and the religious world, or see where the one begins and the other ends.

But God has put these three things forever asunder, and confuse them now as men may, they are and will be forever separated in God's eternal purpose, in His everlasting Word, and in His unerring judgment.

Having considered the purpose of the Second Advent in relation to the church of God, and to the Jew, let us now look at it in relation to the Gentile.

Here again we must go back to the fountainhead, and see in those prophetic titles of Christ, the Son of Man, the Second Man, and the Last Adam, the history of man's ruin and the hope of the world's regeneration.

We have already seen (sermon 7) that as the Son of Abraham, Jesus is the heir of the land, and that as the Son of David, He is the heir of the throne. So also, as the Son of Man, Jesus is "the heir of the world" (Rom. 4:13), and the "heir of all things" (Heb. 1:2, see also Gen. 1:28, and Ps. 8:4–8).

From the beginning God has shown that He has purposes of blessing for the Gentile as such, "when he divided to the nations, their inheritance, when he separated the Sons of Adam" (Deut. 32:8), and when He announced the promise to Abraham that in him "all the nations of the earth shall be blessed" (Gen. 18:18).

All through the history of Israel there were pledges of this future blessing. Individuals were repeatedly brought in for blessing, yea even into the very line of the Messiah, as Rahab and Ruth. Naaman and many others received foretastes of that blessing. The Passover itself was always free to Gentiles under condition of circumcision (Ex. 12:48–49). Many prophecies also point to the fact that Christ was to be a light to lighten the Gentiles as well as the glory of His people Israel.

But the Gentile has failed as well as the Jew. He has been tried in every condition and has failed in every position in which he was placed. When the elect nation failed to exercise power for the glory of God, then power was committed to the Gentiles. The period during which this power is committed to them is called "the times of the Gentiles"— *times,* in the plural, because of there being many nations as distinguished from the one nation of Israel.

Now as to the beginning, the course, and the issue of these times, we are not left to human records or human reason. History does not transpire merely because the events have been predicted, but rather they are foretold because they were ordained to come to pass. Prophecy, as we have seen (sermon 2), did not originate in the prophet's own unfolding of the mind of God, but God Himself in old time revealed His own will, through holy men by His Spirit. Hence we are not left in ignorance or to our own imaginations; the Word of God is so clear and so necessary that history itself cannot be understood without a knowledge of the prophecy.

The times of the Gentiles, as we have already seen (sermon 5), have no reference to the church of God, because the church is itself taken out from the nations (Acts 15:14). These times, however, cannot but be of the deepest interest to us, seeing that in God's providence our lot is not only cast within their limits, but near, very near to their end.[1]

In the prophecy of Daniel we have the great commanding predictions as to these times, from their beginning to their end. Other prophecies speak of them and refer to them, and they all agree in teaching us that those times are marked by progression.

They are marked by evolution, but it is downward and not upward; rather, it is a devolution! They are marked by progress, but it is progress in corruption; by development, but it is in inferiority.

In the prophecy of Daniel this outline is given us in two parts; one from the human standpoint in Daniel 2, where under the figure of a man in stately proportion they are seen in their succession by a man of the Gentiles; the other from the divine standpoint in Daniel 7 and 8, where by a man of God they are seen in their origin. The one therefore displays their outward appearance to the eye of a man of the world; the other reveals their moral character to the eye of the man of God.

Nebuchadnezzar sees these nations and times of the Gentiles under the outward aspect of glittering gold, shining silver, brilliant brass, and irresistible iron. Daniel sees them as wild beasts ferocious in their nature, cruel in their career. Nebuchadnezzar sees them in a dream, as a stately man in his palace. Daniel sees them in a vision of God, as wild beasts arising out of the waters. For—"man being in honor abideth not, he is like the beasts that perish" (Ps. 49:12). And man apart from God has ever gone, and must ever go, down, down! Even the saint without Christ can do nothing. But man apart from God can do only evil continually. He goes down, as it is here shown, from gold to miry clay; from the noble lion to the nondescript dragon! Yes, man has indeed a free will, but it is ever exercised in opposition to God's will. It is "enmity against God, for it is not subject to the law of God, neither indeed can be" (Rom. 8:7). Man has ever destroyed himself, and his help is found only in God (Hos. 13:9).

Now look at the image. Look first at its values. All tends downward, first gold, then silver, brass, iron, and clay. Look at its weight, its specific gravity.

> Gold is equivalent to - - - - - - 19.3
> Silver is equivalent to - - - - - - 10.51
> Brass is equivalent to - - - - - - - 8.5
> Iron is equivalent to - - - - - - - - 7.6
> Clay is equivalent to - - - - - - - - 1.9

Down, down from 19.3 to 1.9. The image is top-heavy, and the first blow of the mighty stone upon the feet shall shatter its pottery and bring it all down in pieces.

So it is with the beasts, which are all emblazoned on the banners and stamped on the coins of the Gentile nations. But they are wild beasts, and they run rapidly down from the lion to the bear, from the bear to the leopard, and from the leopard to the hybrid monstrosity. All is on the descending scale, all is seen to be growing worse and worse. Those who look for the world to improve and progress until it develops into the Millennial kingdom, must account for this. We all agree that these things are figures, but they are figures of a reality, and that which is represented as an ever increasing descent cannot possibly be the figure for a gradual ascent. At any rate, it was not so interpreted to Daniel by the Holy Spirit. He said to Nebuchadnezzar, "Thou art this head of gold, and after thee shall arise another kingdom inferior to thee" (Dan. 2:38–39).

Yet with all this manifest deterioration, there is a seeming advance in apparent greatness, but it is in reality only weakness. The first empire, Babylon, is seen as one; the second, Medo-Persia, is seen as two; the third, Greece, becomes four (Macedonia, Thrace, Syria, and Egypt); and the fourth, Rome, becomes ten. So there is less and less of that unity which is strength, and more and more of that division and separation which is weakness.

As the image thus declines in all that is great, noble, and precious, so the beasts become more wild and ferocious. Government runs down, down! The first (Babylon), was an autocracy "whom he would he slew; and whom he would he kept alive," (Dan 5:59). The second was a parliament of princes, and the law of the Persian kingdom was stronger than the Persian king (Dan. 6:1, 14, and others). The third (Greece), was a government of oligarchies, while in the fourth (Rome) we see the mingling of the princely iron with the communistic clay, until in our day we see more and more of the clay and less and less of the iron, until good government is the one great want of the age all over the world. Man has been tried and found wanting. He cannot govern himself as an individual apart from God. How then can he do it nationally? No! The descent is from God to the Devil, from Christ to the Antichrist.

This moral descent is not affected by any apparent ascending of civilization. Crime may be less revolting and more refined. Sin may be less gross and more polite. Robbery may become less violent but more subtle: instead of being done on the highway it may be done securely in the office, and in the way of business. But the refined sinner and the vulgar sinner are equally far from the kingdom of God. The flesh is bad. It is the same evil and corrupt nature in the saint as in the sinner, and the more you get of it the worse it is. Did you ever notice the opening words of the sixth chapter of the history of the world, and the sixth chapter of the history of the church? Genesis 6, which tells of the corruption which ended in the flood, begins, "And it came to pass when men began to multiply on the face of the earth" (see Prov. 29:16); Acts 6 begins, "And in those days when the number of the disciples was multiplied, there arose a murmuring." God says, "that which is born of the flesh, is flesh" (John 3:6), and however refined, and cultured, and trained the flesh may be, it can never be changed into or become Spirit.

Even with men as individuals there has been deterioration. In the early ages of the world, men were largely given to study the heavens, and they loved to trace their descent from the gods. In our days they study the earth, and are content to trace their evolution from the mud! And so it will be to the end. Down, down, until the times of the Gentiles be fulfilled, filled to the full, and then evil will come to a head. All the evil will then culminate in one man who is called the Antichrist.

The Scriptures reveal him by many names, but every quality, every attribute, every character, every name and act and sign, marks him as an individual. He is called "the king of fierce countenance" (Dan. 8:23); "the little horn" (Dan. 7:8, etc.); "the prince that shall come" (Dan. 9:26), and so on.

There are three great prophecies concerning him given through Daniel (Dan. 7:7–11; 8:19–26; 11; 12), Paul (2 Thess. 2:3–10), and John (Rev. 13; 17; 19).

The early Christians were not ignorant of these things. Their teachers (unlike the teachers of our day) were not mute concerning them. "Remember ye not (says Paul) that while I was with you, I told you these things" (2 Thess. 2:5). The Scriptures are indeed numerous which speak of this awful but important subject. We cannot even refer to them all, but note this instructive parallel—or rather, contrast—between Christ and Antichrist (See chart on next page).

The time of his manifestation is the same in all three of the great prophecies concerning him. In Daniel 8:23, it is "when transgressors are come to the full." In 2 Thessalonians 2, it is when the apostasy is at its height. In Revelation 13, it is when men shall have renounced God and shall "worship the beast."

In Daniel's prophecy the vision concerning Antichrist is fulfilled at "the time of the end" (Dan. 11:40); in Paul's, in "the day of Lord" (2 Thess. 2:2, RV); in John's, at the day of "the wrath of Almighty God" (Rev. 19:18).

Then, further, the doom of the Antichrist is identical in all three of these prophecies. In Daniel 7:11, 13, he is destroyed by "one like the Son of man" coming in the clouds of heaven. In 2 Thessalonians 2:8, "the Lord shall consume [him] with the spirit of his mouth and shall destroy with the brightness of his coming." In Revelation 19:20, he is "cast alive into a lake of fire burning with brimstone." Thus shall end the Antichrist, and with him shall end the times of the Gentiles.

The Antichrist is the last supreme head of Gentile apostasy, and the whole ends with him. Nebuchadnezzar's image is all "broken to pieces together" (Dan. 2:35). And Daniel's beasts are all united in one nameless ten-headed monster in Revelation 13:1–2. It is upon the toes of the image that the stone falls, and it is upon this God-defying beast that the judgment sits. And with him, all Gentile kings, powers, dominions, governments, and ministries end forever! For it happens "in the days of these kings" (Dan. 2:44) over which the beast rules that this end shall come, at the close of this fourth great wild-beast-world-power.

In Revelation 17:8, it is described as the beast which "was, and is not, and shall be present" (RV mg). In John's

CHRIST	Antichrist
"Cometh from above" (John 3:31).	"Ascendeth out of the bottomless pit" (Rev. 11:7).
"I am come in my Father's name" (John 5:43).	"Shall come in his own name" (John 5:43).
"Humbled himself and became obedient unto death" (Phil. 2:8).	"Exalteth himself above all that is called God, or that is worshiped" (2 Thess. 2:4).
"Came down . . . to do . . . the will of him that sent me" (John 6:38).	"Shall do according to his will" (Dan. 11:36).
"I have glorified thee on the earth" (John 17:4).	"Opened his mouth in blasphemy against God" (Rev. 13:6).
"The good shepherd giveth his life for the sheep" (John 10:11).	"Woe to the idle shepherd that leaveth the flock" (Zech. 11:17).
"God hath highly exalted him and given him a name which is above every name" (Phil. 2:9).	"Whom the Lord shall consume with the spirit of his mouth and shall destroy with the brightness of his coming" (2 Thess. 2:8).
"Shall reign for ever and ever" (Rev. 11:15).	"They shall take away his dominion, to consume and to destroy it unto the end" (Dan. 7:26).
"The Son of God" and "heir of all things" (Heb. 1:2).	"The son of perdition" (2 Thess. 2:3).

day it was at its height, and all the world lay beneath its power: It was. Then imperial Rome sank beneath the flood of the Goths and Vandals; though it survives in the titles, dignities, laws, banners, and coins of the fragments into which it is broken, yet in its one outward imperial form it is not. But it shall be present again. For as John looked, he saw that "his deadly wound was healed: and all the world wondered after the beast" (Rev. 13:3). At its head arises the satanic man, energized from hell (2 Thess. 2:9–11; Rev. 13:2, 13–15). The Scriptures describe him as a gross flatterer, a great statesman, a skillful general, but a vile hypocrite. He will pose as the friend of man; he will be a Nero, a Napoleon, and a pope all in one, and the world will be the subject of a strong delusion and wonder after him. But his doom is certain.

The Son of Man will come forth with the armies of heaven, and He will give the Beast to the burning flame. The great stone shall grind the kingdoms of this world to powder. For that stone and that mountain is Christ. As from the mountain all the gold, silver, brass, and iron are obtained, so from Christ all power is derived,[2] and to Christ all power reverts. All power and government in the earth is only delegated, as its first recipient, Nebuchadnezzar, was so solemnly taught of God. And when the great stone comes forth, it will be the power of the Almighty manifested to make all the kingdoms of the world become the kingdoms of our Lord and of His Christ.

And now the times of the Gentiles are hastening to their end. The world is rushing on to its doom. Its Tubal-cains are working out the engines of destruction for the coming war, while its Jubals are lulling it with deceitful strains, to keep it from Christ, and blind its eyes to the coming Antichrist. But its sentence has been passed and its execution is at hand.

Like Jericho of old it is straitly shut up. The men of war look down from the battlements and reproach and revile those who sound the foolish ram's horns of the Gospel. But meanwhile there is a people in it, though not of it; a generation who have heard of the God of Israel and of His Joshua (Jesus); who have welcomed His messengers and gladly received their message of peace. And there is one house in it which is safe, one house which will stand when the cities of the nations fall. That house is built of living stones, sprinkled with the blood, and protected by the scarlet cord, the token of safety from judgment to come.

Dear friends are you within this house? Are you safely

sheltered by Christ's sure sign and token? Is this your refuge? Soon, soon, will the armies of heaven be here and you will either be in their ranks, or left for the judgment that they will execute. And now "because sentence against an evil work is not executed speedily, therefore the heart of the sons of men is fully set in them to do evil."

> As it was in the days of Lot; they did eat, they drank, they bought, they sold, they planted, they builded; but the same day that Lot went out of Sodom it rained fire and brimstone from heaven, and destroyed them all. Even thus shall it be when the Son of man is revealed (Luke 17:28–30).

Yes! as it was! The trader will be engaged in trade, the laborer in toil, the sinner in sins, all saying "peace, peace," when, suddenly, the Lord shall come, "in flaming fire taking vengeance on them that know not God and that obey not the Gospel of our Lord Jesus Christ."

Oh! to be in that house protected by the scarlet thread—the precious blood—and not left to perish with them that believe not. For the same God that shook that city to the ground, and saved that house, has said, "Yet once more I shake not the earth only, but also heaven. . . . that those things which cannot be shaken may remain" (Heb. 12:26–27).

No flood could come on the earth until Enoch was taken and Noah was safe in the ark. No fire could descend on Sodom until Lot be come out. No destruction could come to Jericho until those to be saved were within that house. Dear friends, may we be thus taken up as Enoch was, and taken out as Lot was, and taken in as was that household, alike freed from all condemnation, alike washed in His most precious blood, alike crowned with honor and glory, and "presented faultless before the throne of his glory, with exceeding joy."

Endnotes

1. See the appendix.
2. Matthew 28:18; Proverbs 8:15; Psalm 62:11.

CHAPTER 9

THE RESURRECTION OF THE JUST AND UNJUST

For as in Adam all die, even so in Christ shall all be made alive. But every man in his own order: Christ the firstfruits; afterward they that are Christ's at his coming. Then cometh the end, when he shall have delivered up the kingdom to God, even the Father (1 Cor. 15:22–24).

In this chapter we have the answer to the question which the apostle says "some man will say, How are the dead raised up?" (1 Cor. 15:35). And we are taught (v. 38) that the answer to all such inquiries is the gift of God, and the power of God.

When the Sadducees put their question concerning the resurrection, Jesus said "ye do err, not knowing the scriptures, nor the power of God" (Matt. 22:29).

This is indeed the answer to all our questions and the solution of all our doubts.

When Nicodemus asked, "How can these things be?" The answer was "God so loved the world, that he gave," (John 3:9, 16). When the woman of Samaria asked, "How is it that thou, being a Jew, askest drink of me?" The answer was, "If thou knewest the *gift* of God . . . thou wouldest have asked of him, and he would have *given* thee living water" (John 4:9–10, italics mine). And so here, when one asks, "How are the dead raised up?" The answer is, "God *giveth* it a body as it hath pleased him" (italics mine). All our inquiries are met, and all our difficulties are removed by the Word of God and by the power of God. Faith in this Word and in this power can alone deal with this and all other mysteries, whether they be incarnation, advent, or resurrection. When the apostles used their reason, instead of faith in God's revelation, they failed to understand the plainest of Christ's prophetic statements. When Paul stood on Mars' Hill and spoke of "the resurrection of the dead," we read that some reasoned and "mocked," while others "believed" and "clave unto him."

We stop not now, however, to speak of resurrection as a fact; for all Christian creeds confess it and assert it. But, rather, we desire to learn what the Scriptures reveal concerning the eras of resurrection, and the order in which that wondrous event shall take place.

In our text, first the assertion is made that as all in Adam die, so all in Christ shall be made alive (v. 22). This is qualified by the statement in the next verse, that it shall be all in due order, "Christ the firstfruits; afterward they that are Christ's at his coming. Then cometh the end, when he shall have delivered up the kingdom to God, even the Father."

The word translated "order" is a military expression, and means a band, rank, brigade, or division of an army. Then we are told that the head of this army is Christ the firstfruits. For He is "the firstborn from the dead; that in all things he might have the preeminence" (Col. 1:18). Christ therefore is the Head, and leads the van of this mighty army.

Then we have the next division: afterward they that are Christ's at His coming. These are "the dead in Christ" (1 Thess. 4:16).

Then the end comes—the last great division of this army, not at Christ's coming, but when He shall have delivered up the kingdom to the Father.

Grace has marked off these grand divisions here, and the separation thus made will continue forever.

Now to see the force of the words *afterward* and *then* we

must refer to the beginning of this very chapter where we have a similar construction: "*After that,* he was seen of above five hundred brethren at once. . . . *After that* he was seen of James; then of all the apostles" (vv. 6–7, italics mine). Here these words convey the fact of a distinct interval between the appearances of the risen Savior. We have the same words again in Mark 4:17, "*afterward,* when affliction or persecution ariseth" (italics mine); and verse 28, "first the blade, *then* the ear, *after that* the full corn in the ear" (italics mine). In all these cases there is necessarily a definite interval.

In our text there are more than 1,850 years between Christ the firstfruits and they that are Christ's at His coming. Why then should any difficulty be raised when Revelation distinctly states that a thousand years will elapse between the resurrection of the first of these two great divisions and the second?

Read Revelation 20:4–6:

> And I saw thrones, and they sat upon them, and judgment was given unto them:1 and I saw the souls of them that were beheaded for the witness of Jesus, and for the word of God,2 and which had not worshiped the beast, neither his image, neither had received his mark upon their foreheads, or in their hands;3 and they lived and reigned with Christ a thousand years.

> But the rest of the dead lived not again until the thousand years were finished. This is the first resurrection. Blessed and holy is he that hath part in the first resurrection: on such the second death hath no power, but they shall be priests of God, and of Christ, and shall reign with him a thousand years.

Some persons interpret this first resurrection as a spiritual quickening of those who are dead in sins, and the second as a real and literal resurrection. But surely this cannot be done, for in one and the same context we have two resurrections mentioned, and they are so blended and so spoken of in exactly the same terms that the meaning of the one must fix and settle the meaning of the other. It would be far easier to take them both as being spiritual than to take one spiritually and the other literally. For you first have the spiritual resurrection, then the literal, and then the spiritual again. Yet the language used and words employed are the same in each case. The Holy Spirit has not given us the slightest hint that there is any such transition in the use of the same words, and not the slightest indication or ground for supposing that identical expressions are used in the same passage in opposite senses. And if the Holy Spirit has not done this, surely we may ask, By what authority are we told that we may do so?

Rather let us see how the Spirit Himself interprets to us this solemn and important Scripture.

1. "I saw the souls of them that were beheaded" (v. 4). Surely the word "beheaded" cannot be spiritualized! It must mean people who had literally had their heads cut off! So that those literally dead are the subjects of this resurrection; their death having been fearfully literal, their resurrection shall also be gloriously literal.

2. "They lived" (v. 4). This must be in reunion with their bodies. For the word so translated is never used in any other connection. "God is not the God of the dead but of the living" are words that were spoken by the Lord "as touching the dead that they rise" (Mark 12:26–27). And the cognate verb runs all through 1 Corinthians 15 in this same sense.

3. "This is the first resurrection" (v. 5). Here the Holy Spirit interprets His own words and states distinctly what He means. The word here translated "resurrection" occurs forty-two times and is used without exception of a literal standing upright of those who have lain dead.[4] In any case, it is never used to denote a spiritual quickening.

4. There are those who are called "the rest of the dead" (v. 5), who live not again until the thousand years are finished, and there are the raised dead who live and reign with Christ during that time. These latter are the dead who are distinctly declared to rise with immortal bodies on whom "the second death hath no power" (v. 6), while the

former are "the rest of the dead" who shall be "cast into the lake of fire" (v. 14). There can be no doubt therefore that these two great classes are the same as the two mentioned in our text, and that a thousand years puts them apart.

Taking the expression in 1 Corinthians 15:24, "Then cometh the end," by itself, there is nothing to tell us what end it is, whether the end of the army divisions, that is, the last or final body, or the end of this present age, or the end of the millennial age. But it is added "when he shall have delivered up the kingdom to God, even the Father." Now in Revelation 20:4 we are expressly told of the first great army division that "they lived and reigned with Christ a thousand years," and as they cannot reign with Christ after He has "delivered up the kingdom" it is clear that the second great division cannot refer to the saints unless this reign has already begun.

If we put the two passages together they stand thus. According to 1 Corinthians 15:23, the saints rise at Christ's coming; then, according to Revelation 20:5, 15, they live and reign with Christ a thousand years, and the rest of the dead live not again until the thousand years are finished, when death and hell give up the dead that are in them, "Then cometh the end, when Christ shall deliver up the kingdom to God, even the Father. . . . that God may be all in all" (1 Cor. 15:24, 28).

Now let us turn to other Scriptures and see that whenever the resurrection is mentioned it fits into this divine order. It does so because the character of those who are raised is clearly defined. Whenever we read of the resurrection of the saints, it is spoken of as a hope and as a glory. All who have part in it are "blessed and holy." They have a resurrection like Christ's "from" that is, *from among*, or *out of* the dead. It is not their right as it was Christ's, but it is conferred upon them through infinite grace. Christ rose in virtue of what He was in Himself; they rise in virtue of what grace has made them. Resurrection was due to Christ because of what He had done; resurrection is due to them because of what has been done for them.

They rise therefore in glory; they are sown in corruption and shall be raised in incorruption; they are sown in dishonor but raised in glory; they are sown in weakness but are raised in power (1 Cor. 15:42–44).

They rise like Christ Himself. Their bodies shall be fashioned like unto His own glorious body (Phil. 3:21). The same Spirit which raised up Christ from the dead shall also quicken their mortal bodies (Rom. 8:11). When they awake it will be with His likeness, and they shall be satisfied (Ps. 17:15).

They are Christ's now and here, born not of the will of man but of God. Conduct does not make them His, for they are His by birth. Their standing is in grace and not of works. They are His also by purchase (Acts 9:28; 1 Peter 1:19); and seven times in John 17 does the Savior declare that they are His by gift. Hence when they fall asleep they are still called "the dead in Christ" (1 Thess 4:16), and when they rise again they are still spoken of as "they that are Christ's at his coming."[5]

No wonder then that the resurrection from the dead becomes the one all-powerful hope of the church, and is bound up inseparably with the Lord's second advent.

It was this that Paul longed for when, in Philippians 3:11, he said, "If by any means I might attain unto the resurrection of the dead." If the wicked dead be raised at the same time we can hardly understand this earnest desire. If all rise at one and the same time, of course he would rise, and there was no cause for such a desire. But if the saints are to rise first, then there is every reason why he should so earnestly long to be among those who on this account are pronounced "blessed and holy." The words which he uses here are important and peculiar, for he takes the ordinary word *resurrection* and prefixes a preposition that means "out of" and repeats the same preposition by itself after it, so that the verse really reads, "If by any means I might attain unto the out-resurrection, that one from among the dead"! But why all this desire, and why this force of language, if all the dead rise together? Why not say "from death" or "from the grave"? instead of "out from among the dead" unless it be to show (as in Rev. 20:5) that "the rest of the dead lived not again until the thousand years were finished."

Surely our Lord referred to the same truth when He said, "The children of this world[6] marry, and are given in marriage: but they which shall be accounted worthy to obtain that world, and the resurrection from the dead, neither marry, nor are given in marriage: neither can they die any more: for they are equal unto the angels; and are the children of God, being the children of the resurrection" (Luke 20:34–36). It is clear that some are not accounted worthy. But the article before and after the word "resurrection," and the preposition "from" or "from among" or "out of," gives the same emphasis on which Paul's hope was based.

We can understand also why the disciples should question "one with another what the rising *from* the dead should mean" (Mark 9:10, italics mine), because here Jesus uses the same preposition before the words "the dead," and thus occasions their perplexity. They would have felt no such difficulty about the fact of a resurrection, or a resurrection *of* dead ones. This truth they were familiar with. Jesus said to Mary, "Thy brother shall rise again," and she replied, "I know that he shall rise again in the resurrection at the last day" (John 11:23–24). But a resurrection "out of" the dead, leaving other dead ones behind, was a new revelation to them and caused the disciples to question among themselves what "from" the dead should mean.

We ought to observe here, as final and conclusive, that whenever this first resurrection of the saints is spoken of, this preposition "out of" or "from among" is always used in the Greek, though not always preserved in the KJV. And further that whenever the resurrection of "the rest of the dead" is mentioned, or the resurrection itself, as a fact, this preposition is not used, and it reads simply "the resurrection of dead ones."

Even in the Old Testament we find the same separation, the same elect resurrection more than hinted at. In Daniel 12:2 we read, "Many of them that sleep in the dust of the earth shall awake, some to everlasting life, and some to shame and everlasting contempt." Here it is more than implied that there are two separate events. Some, those who hear the voice of the Son of God shall live; while some—the rest of the dead, who live not again until the thousand years are finished, sleep on in terrible silence! The children of the resurrection hear that voice and awake, as it is written, "Thou shalt call and I will answer."

This is beautifully set forth in another Old Testament Scripture:

> Like sheep they are laid in the grave; death shall feed on them; and the upright shall have dominion over them in the morning; and their [that is, the rest of the dead] beauty shall consume in the grave from their dwelling [mg *the grave being an habitation for every one of them*]. But God will redeem my soul from the power of the grave: for he shall receive me (Ps. 49:14–15).

Another passage where these two resurrections are sometimes taken as though they occurred at one and the same time is John 5:28–29, "The hour is coming, in the which all that are in the graves shall hear his voice, and shall come forth; they that have done good, unto the resurrection of life; and they that have done evil, unto the resurrection of damnation." The word "hour" in verse 28, is the same as in verse 25. But in verse 25 it refers to the time of spiritual quickening of those who are dead in sins. It "now is" says Christ. It is, and has been for at least 1,850 years and will end at Christ's coming. The second hour has not yet begun, and hence it does not say "and now is," but merely, "the hour is coming." This second hour, it might be therefore inferred, would be prolonged, but Revelation 20:4–5 plainly tells us that it will be a thousand years. At the moment of its striking, "the resurrection of life" will take place, and at the moment of its ending will take place the "resurrection of damnation (RV *judgment*).[7]

Then note how the two terms "resurrection of life" and "resurrection of judgment" agree with Revelation 20:4–6. Indeed, Revelation 20 is the great formal and categorical statement, and it is remarkable how the multitude of fragmentary references all fit into it. We have seen how

1 Corinthians 15 so fits in; now look at John 5:28–29. In John 5:28, "they that have done good, unto the resurrection of life"; and Revelation 20:4, "they lived and reigned with Christ a thousand years." In John 5:28, "they that have done evil, unto the resurrection of judgment"; and Revelation 20:13, "they were judged every man according to their works." So with Luke 20:34–36. In Luke 20:34, "neither can they die any more"; and Revelation 20:6, "On such the second death hath no power." In Luke 20:35, "they which shall be accounted worthy to obtain . . . the resurrection from the dead"; and Revelation 20:6, "Blessed and holy is he that hath part in the first resurrection."

What can the Savior mean by all this, if all are compelled to rise again at one and the same moment? Worthiness to obtain it clearly implies that there are those who are not worthy and will not obtain it.

Look again at Luke 14:13–14. Jesus said, "When thou makest a feast call the poor, the maimed, the lame, the blind: and thou shalt be blessed; for they cannot recompense thee: for thou shalt be recompensed at the resurrection of the just." Why not say, simply, "at the resurrection" without distinguishing it? It is clear that those who heard Him did so distinguish it, for one of them immediately cried out, "Blessed is he that shall eat bread in the kingdom of God" (v. 15). This man evidently connected "the resurrection of the just" with the entering into and the establishment of the kingdom.

But there is another passage which is sometimes not thus clearly distinguished, 2 Timothy 4:1, "I charge thee therefore before God, and the Lord Jesus Christ, who shall judge the quick and the dead and *by* his appearing and his kingdom,"not "at" as in the KJV but "and by" as in the RV. This correction, made not by me for the support of our subject, but quite independently by the revisers, not only relieves this passage from any apparent contradiction, but causes it to add its important testimony. First Thessalonians 4:16 is another Scripture. It is fragmentary. It speaks only of "the dead in Christ" but it is in complete agreement with that part of Revelation 20 to which it refers.

In Acts 24:15, Paul again expresses his faith in, and hope of the resurrection of the just, which he distinctly separates from the resurrection of the unjust when he declares "there shall be a resurrection of the dead, both of the just and unjust."

It was this hope that sustained those worthies of faith: Hebrews 11:35, "others were tortured, not accepting deliverance; that they might obtain a better resurrection."

Dear friends, I have thus gone through most, if not all, of the Scriptures which bear on this solemn and important doctrine. You all profess to believe in the resurrection every time you repeat one or other of our creeds. But do you reflect on the bearing that this great doctrine has on yourselves? You have heard of the blessedness of those who have part in the first resurrection and of the doom of the rest of the dead. Oh, what an affecting thought that all of us must have our part in one or the other of these, either in the glories of the first resurrection or in the terrors of the second death! You cannot have part in both.

Surely you have not listened to these solemn Scriptures unmoved! Our Lord speaks, in Luke 20:35, of those who "shall be accounted worthy to obtain that age, and the resurrection from the dead." Oh! to be thus accounted worthy! What does it mean? Who are they that are thus worthy when all our lives we have been unprofitable servants! When we write ourselves down as guilty sinners, vile, and undone, where is our merit? Where is our worthiness? Ah! blessed be God, all who take this ground, the ground of sinners guilty before God, and cry with the publican, "God be merciful to me, a sinner" go down to their houses justified and worthy. With them all merit is forever shut out, and all boasting forever excluded. All the worthiness of Jesus at once becomes theirs—all the worthiness of His life; all the worthiness of His death; all the worthiness of His person and His work! They are worthy in Him and in Him alone.

> Worthy the Lamb is heaven's cry,
> Worthy the Lamb our hearts reply!

Oh, the wondrous worthiness of Jesus! And what a fact for us to remember, that all whom God thus *accounts* worthy, He *makes* worthy! Jesus was made sin for them, and they are made the righteousness of God in Him; though in their own estimation they are still worthless, and they feel themselves to be increasingly so day by day, yet their desire is to live for God, to walk with God, to look for the Savior, to love His appearing, and to rejoice in the hope of the first resurrection.

Dear friends, these are not mere sentiments or opinions. May God give us to see the importance and solemnity of them as great facts. May you be led to see that he who talks about these things and repeats them in a creed, and yet knows not the power of them, does but deceive himself and goes into eternity with a lie in his right hand. May God lay this great subject on all our hearts that we may increasingly desire with Paul that "if by any means we might attain to the out-resurrection from among the dead," and for this to count all else but dross. The Lord grant it, for Christ's sake.

Endnotes

1. These already enthroned appear to be the church (1 Cor. 6:2) which, like Christ Himself, is "a kind of firstfruits of his creatures" (James 1:18), and is hence called the "church of the firstborn," i.e.—the firstborn from the dead. The term *firstborn* cannot be used in opposition to the *unsaved*, but to others who are *born*, though not "firstborn."
2. These are the souls seen slain in Revelation 6:9, but are now seen resurrected, for it says in 20:4 "they lived."
3. These are their fellow servants and brethren who in Revelation 6:2 were alive but were yet to be killed as they had been; and *were* killed in Revelation 13:7, 15; 14:12–13, and seen raised in vision in 15:2.

   Thus there appear to be three subdivisions of this great "first" division, and though the definite acts of such resurrections from among the dead and ascensions of living ones are not mentioned, they are more than implied, if not necessitated, by the various visions of the apocalypse. Those raised in Matthew 27:52–53, must also be included in this "first resurrection."

4. Unless Luke 2:34 be an exception, "This child is set for the fall and rising again of many in Israel."

5. Those who hold that any of the members of Christ's body, the church, will be left behind to pass through the Great Tribulation or any part of it (1) fail to see how completely the members of His body are His by birth and covenant relation, and not by conduct; and (2) are not clear as to the sense in which they use the word *church*. It is by no means necessary to include those who will pass through and be saved out of the Great Tribulation in "the church." The church will not include *all* the saved.

6. RV mg "*Age.*"

7. You have the same joining together of events that are widely separate in their occurrence in Isaiah 61:1. And you have the divine exegesis of Christ in Luke 4:19.

CHAPTER 10

THE JUDGMENT OF THE QUICK AND THE DEAD

We must all appear before the judgment seat of Christ (2 Cor. 5:10).

When the son of man shall come in his glory, and all the holy angels with him, then shall he sit upon the throne of his glory: and before him shall be gathered all nations: and he shall separate them one from another, as a shepherd divideth his sheep from the goats (Matt. 25:31–32).

And I saw a great white throne, and him that sat on it, from whose face the earth and the heaven fled away; and there was found no place for them. And I saw the dead, small and great, stand before God; and the books were opened: and another book was opened, which is the book of life: and the dead were judged out of those things which were written in the books, according to their works. . . . And whosoever was not found written in the book of life was cast into the lake of fire (Rev. 20:11–12, 15).

Our next subject is the judgment of the quick—the living—and the dead." I have used this expression because it is in the words of Scripture (2 Tim. 4:1), and also because it is a term we are accustomed to use in all our creeds.

The word *judgment* does not, of itself, necessarily include rewards and punishments, for it is often used simply of rule and government. Hence, as characteristic of Christ's future glorious reign on earth we read, "He shall judge thy people with righteousness, . . . He shall judge the poor of the people" (Ps. 72:2, 4), and again, "He shall judge the world with righteousness, and the people with his truth" (Ps. 96:13).

The whole of this righteous rule is called the Day of the Lord because it will be the day of the Lord's judgment. The present day is called man's day[1] (1 Cor. 4:3, and mg) because it is the day when men judge one another, but another day is coming when the Lord shall be the judge. That day opens with judgment, judgment runs through it, and judgment closes it.

All governments have their judicial departments, and so this future government of the Lord will have its definite judicial seasons and occasions. The three Scriptures that I have just read bring before us three definite and distinct judgment scenes.

In connection with this, it is interesting and important to note that the Lord Jesus Christ is the executor of all judgment. He was unjustly judged by man, and He shall be the judge of men. The scene of His rejection shall be the scene of His triumph.

The Scriptures are very explicit on this point:

> He hath appointed a day, in the which he will judge the world in righteousness by that man whom he hath ordained; whereof he hath given assurance unto all men, in that he hath raised him from the dead (Acts 17:31).

> The Father judgeth no man, but hath committed all judgment unto the Son (John 5:22).

It is as the Son of God that He raises the dead, but it is as the Son of Man that He executes judgment (see John 5:25, 27).

The whole question of judgment is founded on the immutable purpose of God, the infinite knowledge of God, and the infallible Word of God. None can question His power; none can doubt His truth. "Hath he said and shall he not do it? hath he spoken, and shall he not make it good?"

As to the times of these judgments, it is written "to everything there is a season, and a time to every purpose under heaven. . . . God shall judge the righteous and the wicked: for there is a time there for every purpose and for every work" (Eccl. 3:1, 17). All is ordained and ordered by God.

And here let us again put each other in remembrance that this is not a question of human opinion, nor is it a question as to any difference of opinion, but it is wholly a question of revelation. If we know all that the Scriptures say about it, then we know all that can be known. If we do not know all that the Scriptures say, then we must err for it is written, "Ye do err, not knowing the Scriptures nor the power of God." There have been and there are schools of theology, systems of doctrine, shades of thought, but if this is all the doctrine is, then man may do as he pleases about it, accept it or reject it, or believe concerning it just what he likes. But if God has spoken, then there is an end of all argument. We have only to bow and believe.

Now let us see what God has been pleased to reveal concerning judgment in these three Scriptures.

2 Corinthians 5:10

A judgment is spoken of in 2 Corinthians 5:10, "We must all appear before the judgment seat of Christ."

1. Who are they that appear in this judgment scene? The apostle answers "We." Who are the we? And the answer is clear, We who "labor that . . . we may be accepted of him" (v. 7); we who "walk by faith" (v. 7); we who have "the earnest of the Spirit" (v. 5); we, Paul and Timothy, by whom the epistle was written, and "the church of God" and "all the saints" (2 Cor. 1:1). In fact it is impossible to find any but the saints of God in this Scripture.

2. Why do we appear? The apostle answers, "To be made manifest." To "receive." For what? For deeds done, service rendered, and works wrought—even as he had taught them in his first epistle. He is speaking here of those who build on the one foundation which is Jesus Christ, and he says,

> Now if any man build upon this foundation gold, silver, precious stones, wood, hay, stubble; every man's work shall be *made manifest* [the very expression used in our text]: for the day shall declare it, because it shall be revealed by fire; and the fire shall try every man's work of what sort it is. If any man's work abide which he hath built thereupon, *he shall receive* a reward. If any man's work be burned, he shall suffer loss: but *he himself shall be saved*; yet so as by fire (1 Cor. 3:12–15).

Can any one doubt that we have the same scene here as in our text? We have the same object stated, and the same expression used, the works "shall be made manifest." We have also the same result, "he shall receive" according to the work. If it is good, he shall receive a reward. If it is bad, the work will be burned up, but the worker or builder shall be saved.

3. Where do we appear to be made manifest? The apostle answers before the *Bema* of Christ. The Bema was in one sense a judgment seat. It was not the seat of a judge who gave judicial sentences, punishments, and acquittals, but it was a raised daïs from which the judge gave the crowns to the victors in the public games. It was for such a crown the apostle labored, ran, and fought, and when reviewing that service he said:

> Henceforth there is laid up for me a crown of righteousness, which the Lord, the righteous Judge, shall give me at that day: and not to me only, but unto all them also that love His appearing (2 Tim. 4:8).

Thus, there is no judgment at all in the common sense of the word, but an awarding of crowns and rewards for acceptable service. The recipients are already accepted in the Beloved as to their persons, and therefore they strive to be acceptable as to their service. As to their standing, they appear there in all the righteousness of Christ, perfect in all His perfection, glorious in all His glory, beautiful in all His beauty, raised in His likeness, conformed to His image, and made like His own body of glory! How then can they be judged to see if they are lost or saved? The very feeblest of them have already been judged in the person of their Substitute. He bore their sin. He has undergone all the judgment due to them, and hence all who are quickened with Christ are said to be "risen with Christ" so that the question of sin can never again be opened. "To them that look for him shall he appear, without sin, unto salvation" (Heb. 9:28).[2]

For all such, death is sleep, through Jesus; for it is not necessary that they should die because this penalty of sin has been paid. Therefore, those who are alive and remain to Christ's coming will not die at all. And as to judgment, it is positively stated by Jesus Himself that they "shall not come into judgment" (John 5:24).[3] Hence the apostle asks, "Who shall lay anything to the charge of God's elect? Shall God that justifieth? Who is he that shall condemn? Shall Christ that died?"[4] To suppose that one of God's saints could ever come into judgment as to his standing and his title to glory is not only to flatly contradict the direct statement of Christ Himself, but it is to deny the very foundations of the Gospel; it is to rob the work of Christ of all its merit! For not only does Christ assert the contrary, but the Holy Spirit in Romans 8:1 also expressly declares, "There is now no condemnation to them that are in Christ Jesus."

Do you not see that if our title to glory and our standing in righteousness was not settled at the Cross, it is not settled now! that if we did not die with Christ we must die for sin ourselves! that if our salvation is not settled now it must be settled in judgment! and if it has to be settled then, there can be only one result, for it is written, "Enter not into judgment with thy servant, O Lord, for in thy sight shall no man living be justified" (Ps. 143:2). It may sound very humble to say "we cannot know we are saved until the day of judgment," but this is the essence of Romanism, and he who says it knows nothing of the Gospel, nothing of the work of Christ, nothing of the results of His atonement. He who says it may call those who rejoice in these precious truths presumptuous, but when Christ says, "He that heareth my word, and believeth on him that sent me, hath everlasting life, and shall not come into condemnation [judgment]; but is passed from death unto life" (John 5:24), then we maintain that it is presumption to deny it and not to believe it! Those who, in spite of all their conviction of sin, set to their seal that God is true, are truly *humble*, while those who profess to be too humble thus to believe His Word are really guilty of presumption!

All who are in Christ are saved, justified, and sheltered from all judgment. They are risen with Christ and stand with Christ on resurrection ground. They hope for the resurrection of life, endless glory, and eternal blessedness in the presence of God and the Lamb.

But their work has yet to be appraised, their works have yet to be assayed, their service has yet to be tried; hence "we shall all stand before the *Bema* of Christ" (Rom. 14:9–13). We shall then see how little of our service has been done for the glory of God, and how much for the praise of men; how little with the single eye, and how much with a second motive; how little "fulfilled before God" (Rev. 3:2), and how much before our fellows. And while much, or most, and in many cases all, will be burnt up; yet all who stand there in that heavenly scene will be saved.

Matthew 25:31–33

A judgment is spoken of in Matthew 25:31–33, "When the Son of man shall come in his glory, and all the holy angels with him, then shall he sit upon the throne of his glory: and before him shall be gathered all nations: and he shall separate them one from another, as a shepherd divideth his sheep from the goats: and he shall set the sheep on his right hand, but the goats on the left."

The popular belief concerning this Scripture is that we have here what is called "the general judgment," in which all who have ever lived or died shall stand. But observe:

1. There is not a word said about resurrection. We may at least put the presumption that there will not be one, against the assumption that there will be one.

2. Who are they that thus gathered? It says "all nations." The word here translated "nations" occurs one hundred and fifty times in the New Testament, and it is never used of any but nations actually existing as such. It occurs with the article, as in our text, one hundred and thirty-two times; it is rendered "the gentiles," ninety-two times; "the nations," ten times; "the heathen," five times; and simply "nations," twenty-five times. Now is it too much to ask, that if in Matthew 25:32 the more usual translation, "the Gentiles,"had been given, would the current belief have been as popularly held? If it had been rendered, as it is ninety-two times out of a hundred and thirty-two, "Before him shall be gathered all the Gentiles"—would the popular belief have obtained the hold that it has?

3. Where shall all the nations be gathered? In answering this question we must note that there are many prophecies in which similar expressions are used, which point to the conclusion that the very same event is probably intended. When we look at them we must be struck with the fact that God will deal by and by with the nations (or the Gentiles) as such. We read:

Come near, ye nations, to hear; and hearken, ye people: let the earth hear, and all that is therein; the world, and all things that come forth of it. For the indignation of the LORD is upon all nations (Isa. 34:1–2).

For, behold, in those days, and in that time, when I shall bring again the captivity of Judah and Jerusalem, I will also gather all nations, and will bring them down into the valley of Jehoshaphat, and will plead with them there for my people and for my heritage Israel, whom they have scattered among the nations, and parted my land. . . . Assemble yourselves, and come, all ye heathen, and gather yourselves together round about: thither cause thy mighty ones to come down, O LORD. Let the heathen be wakened, and come up to the valley of Jehoshaphat: *for there will I sit to judge all the heathen* round about" (Joel 3:1–2, 11–12, italics mine).

And I will set my glory among the heathen, and all the heathen shall see my judgment that I have executed, and my hand that I have laid upon them (Ezek. 39:21).

4. It is important and material to be clear as to the fact that the church of God will not stand in that gathering.

    a.   It is written that God is now visiting "the Gentiles, to take out of them a people for his name" (Acts 15:14). If the church is taken out of the nations, it surely cannot be included in the nations, or be judged with them.

    b.   We have already heard the words of Christ, how He said, he that heareth my word, and believeth on Him that sent me, hath everlasting life, and shall not come into judgment (John 5:24).

5. It is also clear that the Jew cannot be in this judgment of the nations, for it is expressly declared that the Jews "shall not be reckoned among the nations" (Num. 23:9). So that if the Jew be not there, and the church of God be not there, then it is certain that it can be only the Gentile.

6. Look at the ground of the judgment. The popular belief is that the sheep are the just, and the goats are the unjust. But there is a third party, whom the judge calls "my brethren," with reference to which both sheep and goats are judged. How can this be a general judgment if there are three parties and one of them is not included in it? The two parties are judged as to how they received and treated the third. Surely this cannot refer to any who have lived in this dispensation of the grace of God. Surely those who now reject Christ and His salvation will have something more to answer for than not caring for and tending the Jew; those who are saved in Christ with an everlasting salvation will have a very different title to glory than that furnished by their own works. Even infidels have not been slow to see this point, and to urge it against the Bible and Christianity.

7. The reward is also peculiar. It is "the kingdom prepared for them from the foundation of the world." When the church of God is mentioned in this connection, it is "before the foundation of the world" (Eph. 1:4; John 17:24; 1 Peter 1:20). This is the expression that is used of the Christ of God and the church of God because it is the heavenly, eternal, and everlasting kingdom with which they stand connected. Here in Matthew 25 it is an earthly kingdom; it is the kingdom "under the whole heaven," for "the earth hath he given to the children of men" (Ps. 115:16). The title to "the everlasting kingdom of God's dear Son," the kingdom of priests, is a title all of grace, and only of grace. But the title to the kingdom "under the whole heaven," the kingdom "from" the foundation of the world, is a title of peculiar works with reference to the Lord's brethren the Jews.

Thus the ways of God in judgment are righteous, and suited to the conditions of His own divisions of humanity—"the Jew, the Gentile, and the church of God."

All that is revealed to us of Israel, and the ways of God; all that we know of God's purposes, counsels, and thoughts; all that we know of Christ, His person and His work; all that we know of the church of God, her calling and standing before God, her completeness in Christ, her acceptance in the Beloved, and her title to glory; and all that we know of the Scriptures of truth forbid us to include either the church of God or the Israel of God. Israel will be restored, saved and blessed. As for the church, are we asked to believe that God justifies her now by grace and will judge her then by works? That He will blot out her transgressions now, and condemn her for them then? That He will again bring her sins in remembrance, when He has said "their sins and their iniquities will I remember no more"?

8. Having thus seen who they are not, it may be well to look more closely at who they are who are to stand in this judgment. It appears from Acts 15:16–17, quoted from Amos 9:11–12, that after the ascension of the church and her return to Christ, and the restoration of Israel, there will be a "residue" of the Gentiles who will enter into blessing.

We read that when the taking out of the church from among the Gentiles shall have been completed:

> After this I will return, and will build again the tabernacle of David, which is fallen down; and I will build again the ruins thereof, and I will set it up: that the residue of men might seek after the Lord, *and all the Gentiles*, upon whom my name is called, saith the Lord, who doeth all these things (Acts 15:16–17; see Amos 9:11–12).

May not this residue be the sheep referred to here? And as for the goats, are they not included in those who are dealt with in Daniel 7:26–27?

> The judgment shall sit. . . . And the kingdom and dominion, and the greatness of the kingdom under the whole heaven, shall be given to the people of the saints of the most High.

May not this be the very judgment here spoken of and referred to in 2 Timothy 4:1 as the judgment of "the quick," that is, the living at Christ's appearing and His kingdom; and described more at length in Revelation 19:11–21?

9. All this is clearly before the Millennium and upon the earth. It is when the Son of Man shall sit upon the throne of His glory, which is the throne of His father David, and when He shall appear with His holy angels "to execute judgment" (Jude 15; see Zech. 14:5; 2 Thess. 2:8).

10. But even this judgment is neither total nor final, for after the Millennium, Satan will be loosed, as we read in Revelation 20:7–10. The nations again revolt and are destroyed on the earth by fire sent down from heaven, while the Devil who deceived them is then dealt with finally and forever. And now one word as to the reality of this judgment. If words are to have any definite meaning then we have finality as to those who are here judged and sentenced. The expressions are definite, and the words are precise; the issues are tremendous, and the results are final! The same word, "eternal," is used by the Judge Himself of both destinies, and all who receive the Bible as the

inspired revelation of God's will, must receive them as absolute, final, and authoritative.

Revelation 20:11–15

A judgment is spoken of in Revelation 20:11–12, 15, "And I saw a great white throne, and him that sat on it, from whose face the earth and the heaven fled away; and there was found no place for them. And I saw the dead, small and great, stand before God; and the books were opened: and another book was opened, which is the book of life: and the dead were judged out of those things which were written in the books, according to their works. . . . And whosoever was not found written in the book of life was cast into the lake of fire."

This is the great and final judgment scene, and here we must notice:

1. That the time of this judgment is after the thousand years have ended.

2. The place of this great white throne is not on this earth. In this it is similar to the appearance of the saints, in 2 Corinthians 5, which is in the heavens, though before the *Bema* of Christ. It is distinguished from "the throne" in Matthew 25, for that is on the earth, while here it is distinctly stated that "the earth and heaven fled away, and there was found no place for them" (Rev. 20:11).

3. The persons who are here judged are all of them raised from the dead for this special purpose. Hence it is called in John 5:29, "the resurrection of, damnation [judgment]," as distinguished from "the resurrection of life." There shall not be one before this throne who has not died. In this it differs from both the other judgment scenes, for in the first (2 Cor. 5), only "those which are alive and remain" and "the dead in Christ" then raised will be there; in the second (Matt. 25), only living nations, for resurrection is not even hinted at. Those who introduce "the dead" into the judgment of the living nations (Matt. 25) do not hesitate to introduce the living among those who are here called the dead! But they have no more authority for the one than for the other.

4. The judgment itself is one of standing and character.

It is "according to their works" (vv. 12–13), not to discover good works which may be rewarded, or dead works which may be burned up and the workers saved, but to punish wicked works that manifest the character of the workers as the enemies of God.

5. One question arises here, and that is, are any found in this judgment who are rewarded and saved? The answer is, that not a word is said about it, and where God has not spoken we must hold our peace. All we can say is that the omission is very strange and unaccountable if this be a general judgment of good and bad. The fact of its being called "the resurrection of judgment" as distinguished from "the resurrection of life" seems to imply that all who are thus raised are for condemnation. True, the Lamb's Book of Life is opened, but it does not say that the names of any who are judged are found therein. There is not a word about any arraignment, there is no pleading, no defense; all are speechless.

The description seems to include the wicked dead of every age for "the sea gave up the dead which were in it; and death and the grave (mg) delivered up the dead which were in them: and they were judged every man according to their works" (Rev. 20:13).

It does not say that any whose names were in the Book of Life were here. It does not say that there were any who were not cast into the lake of fire, which is the second death.

While Scripture is silent on this particular point, and where this is so we may not speak with certainty, yet on one point all is certain: this judgment is absolute and final. There is no reprieve, and no release. There is no room here for the newly invented fiction of a Protestant purgatory, or for the new theory of "eternal hope." It may be found in human theology, but it is not found in God's Word, and it is a bold interpolator who dares to insert any hope in the words of this Scripture. To attempt it is to repeat the lie of Satan and say "ye shall not surely die"! How can there be room for repentance then, when the call to repent today is based on the very fact that there will be none after death?

God "now commandeth all men everywhere to repent: because he hath appointed a day, in the which he will judge the world in righteousness," (Acts 17:30–31). The very fact of there being a judgment to come is the reason why people are commanded to repent now.

The great and important question for us now and here is, have you repented now? and are you sheltered from this judgment? Its portion is yours if you are not washed in the blood of the Lamb. If you have not your part in the first resurrection, the resurrection of life, then you must have it in the resurrection of judgment. That judgment will not be like the judgments of this world. These are generally limited in their scope and defective in their operation. They are often evaded by technicalities, perverted by bribes, and eluded by deceit. But not so with that judgment. Oh, how solemn. Is it possible that any can have heard these truths and be unmoved? Can it be that any are still heedless? Oh, how awful to be sporting on the brink of a grave that will never open until this great white throne shall be set!

You have seen clearly that only those who are Christ's now, who have heard His Word, and believed on Him that sent Him "shall not come into judgment." Have you heard? Do you believe? Oh, what momentous questions— questions on which eternal destinies hang! Better far discover your true state and condition before God now than to find it out when it will be forever too late. Better far come now to the throne of grace and obtain mercy than to stand before that throne of judgment and find the second death! May it be yours, now, to find the Lord gracious and merciful, while yet He tarries, for the long-suffering of God is salvation. May it be yours to be sheltered by His precious blood, and not come into judgment.

I cannot conclude without thanking God for the privilege of being called to bear this testimony for Him and His Word. I pray that a rich blessing may rest upon it, and that many may be awakened to take a greater interest in prophetic truth; to see its importance; to contend earnestly for the faith once delivered to the saints; to have their *love* increased for a crucified Savior, their *faith* increased in a risen Savior, and their *hope* increased for a coming Savior.

Endnotes

1. It is important to notice these definite expressions of God's Word.
   a. Man's day (1 Cor. 4:3), is this present time; and it runs on until
   b. The day of Christ (Phil. 1:6, 10; 2:16), which is the day of Christ's presence with His saints in the heavenlies, where their service is assayed, their crowns awarded, and the marriage of the Lamb celebrated. In *heaven* it is the "day of Christ" but on *earth* it is the day of Antichrist; and that day runs on until
   c. The Day of the Lord, when He comes with His saints, to judge and rule and reign for a thousand years; and this day runs on until
   d. The Day of God (2 Peter 3:12), at the close of the Millennium, when Christ delivers up the kingdom to God even the Father "that God may be all in all" (1 Cor. 15:24–28). See my pamphlet on this subject, "Four Prophetic Periods."
2. RV "So Christ also, having been once offered to bear the sins of many, shall appear a second time, apart from sin, to them that look for him, unto salvation."
3. This is the meaning of the word here translated "condemnation," and rendered "judgment" in the RV. It occurs forty-eight times, and is forty-one times translated "judgment."
4. So the RV margin, and Tregelles.

A P P E N D I X

THE BEGINNING OF THE END

When it is evening, ye say, it will be fair weather: for the sky is red. And in the morning, it will be foul weather today: for the sky is red and lowering. O ye hypocrites, ye can discern the face of the sky; but can ye not discern the signs of the times? (Matt. 16:2–3).

These are the words of the Lord Jesus when the Pharisees and Sadducees asked for "a sign from heaven." He declared (v. 4) that no such sign would be given and that nothing should be added to the signs of the prophetic word.

There were then Jews who did discern these signs of the Word and were looking and waiting for His first coming.

At Christ's second coming there shall be signs from heaven, great and terrible, but we have already and now the signs of the sure word of prophecy. We desire in this appendix to show from these signs of the Scriptures that we are fast approaching the time when there shall appear the sign of the Son of Man in heaven.

The Second Advent of Christ

The second advent of Christ will consist of a series of events of which the visible and personal appearing of Christ will be the great central point. His first coming consisted of many events, and extended over a period of about thirty-three years. A Jew read of this coming in Micah 5:2, "thou Bethlehem Ephratah . . . out of thee shall he come forth unto me that is to be ruler in Israel," and he also read of this same coming in Zechariah 9:9, "Rejoice greatly, O daughter of Zion; shout, O daughter of Jerusalem; behold, thy King cometh unto thee." But there was nothing in these prophecies to tell him that there were to be more than 30 years between these two events, which were both Christ's coming. So likewise in the prophecies of Christ's second coming, we read, "I will come again and receive you unto myself" (John 14:3); and, "The Lord my God shall come, and all the saints with thee." There is nothing to tell us how long an interval will elapse between the reception of the saints by Christ, and their coming with Him in glory, though some interval is clearly implied. And so when we read that the saints are to be caught up "to meet the Lord in the air" (1 Thess. 4:17), there is nothing to tell us how long they shall be with Him there before they return with him in glory; whether it is to be momentary or prolonged. We learn, however, from many Scriptures that at least seven years will run their course, for this period is spoken of several times in its various parts of 1,260 days, 42 months, and 3 1/2 years. Whether it will be extended beyond this we are not told. All the events that are recorded in the book of "The Revelation of Jesus Christ" are connected with, and form part of that revelation, and go to make up the Second Advent, while the personal appearing of Christ will of course form a definite act in that series of events, as definite as the lightning's flash.

If this consideration be borne in mind it will solve many difficulties and remove many perplexities. So with our next topic.

The Return of the Jews

The return of the Jews will not be accomplished in a day or a week. But as we have seen in sermon number 8, there will be a preliminary, or partial, or natural gathering; there will be also a "second" complete and miraculous gathering.

The return from Babylon occupied more than forty years. The rebuilding of the street and the wall was to be in "the strait of times" (Dan. 9:25, mg), that is, the smaller interval of the two named, in "seven weeks," or seven sevens of years, that is, forty-nine years. The dispersion of the Jews likewise was not completed until the destruction of Jerusalem, forty years after Christ foretold it in Luke 21. So we might expect the gathering of the Jews to their city and land to be accomplished gradually in the course of years, and by apparently natural causes: when the Antichrist shall be revealed in his time and, first by flatteries and deceit, then by violence and persecution, shall lead up to his own destruction by the glory of Christ's coming with His saints—the saints having been previously caught up to meet Him in the air.

In a work by the Reverend Dr. S. H. Kellog, of Pennsylvania, entitled, *"The Jews: Or Prediction and Fulfillment,"*[1] there is a mass of evidence and a collection of facts showing how in the past history of the Jews the most minute predictions have been literally fulfilled, and pointing the most powerful argument to a like literal fulfillment of prophecies in the present and in the near future. We must refer those who wish to go more deeply into the subject to Dr. Kellog's book, while we give a brief *résumé* of his facts and figures in the following notes.

In showing that predictions as to the future of Israel are already beginning to receive their fulfillment, it is not necessary to assert or to assume that God has begun to deal with the Jews in the proper sense of the term. God has not now two distinct peoples on the earth under two distinct covenants, any more than He had in the early years of the church when the Jews were being dispersed. In the Acts of the Apostles we see how the church of God was being formed and, side by side with that, the Jews were being scattered and dispersed and the temple destroyed, according to the Word of God. All through this dispensation predictions have been receiving their fulfillment. Prophecies are in the same way being now fulfilled in our own day, and this is fast leading up to the time when God will again put forth His hand to deal with His people Israel and remove His church to be "forever with the Lord."

In order to appreciate the facts that Dr. Kellog marshals as to this present fulfillment, it is necessary to read carefully such prophecies of the past eighteen hundred years as Deuteronomy 28:25, 63–64, and think of the millions of Jews destroyed in the siege of Jerusalem and in the revolts of A.D. 116 and 135, etc. So also Deuteronomy 28:29, 43, 48, all have been literally fulfilled, and verses 58–59, where God said He would make their plagues "wonderful" and "of long continuance," and that "the stranger . . . shall get up above thee very high; and thou shalt come down very low" (v. 43). For two thousand years God has watched over them to destroy them, and now if we see predictions being fulfilled under our eyes, it is because God is watching over them to accomplish His Word, although He may not yet have actually commenced to deal with them as with His people again.

As to the past fulfillment of Deuteronomy 28 we have to remember that under pagan Rome their lot was hard, and under papal Rome it was harder still. Constantine began the oppression, and Justinian continued it by expressly excluding the Jews from his code. Ever since then the Jews have been the objects of unreasoning and pitiless hatred; the victims of repeated confiscations, violence, torture, massacres, and banishments. From the time of the Crusades the Jews have been legally plundered, and brief respites have been dearly paid for. In 1290 they were expelled from England, in 1395 from France, and in 1492 from Spain. The Reformation only mitigated their sufferings, for the Protestant Princes subjected the Jews to live in separate quarters; to wear a distinctive dress; to submit to exceptional legislation; while they were the subjects of systematic indignity, insult, and oppression.

Hosea 3:4; Leviticus 26:31; Isaiah 61:4; 32:13–15; Micah 3:12, have all been literally fulfilled, and so has Luke 21:24, which says that "Jerusalem shall be trodden down of the Gentiles until the times of the Gentiles be fulfilled." Attempts have been made to falsify this prediction. In A.D. 362, Julian the apostate tried it in vain. In 1799

Napoleon I tried to settle the Jews there, but he failed. Pagans have held Jerusalem, Christians have held it, Mahommedans have held it, but the Jews, never since that word went forth, and will not, "until the times of the Gentiles be fulfilled."

Now look at seven great predictions that stand in direct contrast to all those we have just named, a contrast so great that nothing else could explain the facts that we see transpiring before our eyes, or reveal the causes of the marvelous transformation in the condition of the Jews during this present century.

1. *The breaking of the Gentile yoke* (Jer. 30:8). "It shall come to pass in that day,[2] saith the Lord of hosts, that I will break his [the Gentile's] yoke from off thy neck, and will burst thy bonds, and strangers shall no more serve themselves of him." When we think of the eighteen hundred years and more during which that heavy yoke has been borne and the bonds with which the Jews have been bound, is it too much to see in recent events the beginning of the end of the oppression of ages? Look at the following entirely new facts in the light of that oppression.

   a. In 1783 Joseph II of Austria first abolished the body tax, removed vexatious restrictions, and opened the schools to the Jews.
   b. In 1784 Louis XVI of France abolished the body tax.
   c. In 1787 Frederick William of Prussia repealed some of the laws which Frederick the Great had made.
   d. In 1788 Louis XVI appointed a commission to remodel the laws respecting the Jews. The Revolution stopped this work, but it included the Jews in its liberty, equality, and fraternity.
   e. In 1805 Alexander I of Russia revoked the Edict of Exclusion and millions returned there.
   f. In 1806 they were made citizens of Italy and Westphalia (as they had been some years before of Holland and Belgium), and were formally recognized by Napoleon I as a religious body.

g. In 1809, Baden; and 1823, Prussia and Denmark gave the Jews civil liberty.

h. In England, successive Acts in 1830, 1833, and 1835 removed certain restrictions, but it was not until 1858 that the Jews had full equality.

i. In 1870 Bismarck completed the unification of Germany and made the Jews free all through the empire.

j. In 1867 Turkey gave the Jews, for the first time, the right to possess land in Palestine.

k. In 1870 with the fall of the temporal power of the pope, freedom came in Italy.

l. In 1878 the Berlin Congress made the freedom of the Jews in Romania a special condition.

Is it too much to conclude that in all these things, Jeremiah 30:7 has begun to be fulfilled.

2. *Restoration gradual* (Ezek. 37:7–14). The restoration is not to be the one work of a moment, but it is marked by successive stages. (1) "a noise," (2) "a shaking," (3) "the bones came together, bone to his bone," (4) "the sinews and flesh came up upon them," (5) "the skin covered them above," (6) "the breath came into them and they lived," and (7) they "stood up upon their feet."

Now as the restoration of Israel cannot be the work of a moment or a day, or of a mere brief period, is it too much to ask whether we may not call these present movements, the "noise" and the "shaking," even if not the coming together of bone to bone?

a. In 1806 Napoleon summoned the great Sanhedrim for the first time in Europe.

b. In 1860, "The Alliance Israelite Universelle" was formed in Paris.

c. In later years many other organizations have been formed that may surely be regarded as similar signs.

3. *The transfer of wealth* (Isa. 60:9–10). "Surely the isles

shall wait for me, and the ships of Tarshish first, to bring thy sons from far, their silver and their gold with them" (v. 9).

So also Isaiah 33:1: speaking to the Gentiles God says, "Woe to thee that spoilest, and thou wast not spoiled; and dealest treacherously, and they dealt not treacherously with thee! when thou shalt cease to spoil, thou shalt be spoiled; and when thou shalt make an end to deal treacherously, they shall deal treacherously with thee." And as to when this shall take place, we learn from verse 10.

Now we cannot properly appreciate the following facts unless we continually bear in mind the condition of the Jews during the last eighteen centuries. There is no lack of evidence to show the gradual accumulation of capital in Jewish hands.

    a. The Rothschilds' loans amount to four million sterling to England, one million to Austria, one million to Prussia, two and a half million to France, one million to Russia, and a quarter of a million to Brazil, ten million altogether.

    b. The Jews are the money lenders of Europe.

    c. In 1869 in Russia 73 percent of the immovable property had passed into Jewish hands, and a quarter of the railway property was in the hands of the Russian railway king, Samuel Solomonowitz de Poliakoff.

    d. The official returns of Prussia, 1861, showed that 38,000 Jews out of 75,000 were engaged in commerce, while only 1 Jew in 586 was a day laborer.

    e. In 1871, out of 642 bankers in Prussia, all but 92 were Jews. Thus while the Jews were only 2 percent of the population, 85 percent of the bankers were Jews.

    f. In 1871 in Berlin, the Jews were only 5 percent of the population, but the employers of labor were 39 percent of the Gentiles, and 71 percent of the Jews, while the merchants were 55 percent of the Jews and only 12 percent of the Gentiles.

    g. In Vienna, the Bourse is almost entirely in Jewish hands.

h. In Lower Austria, out of 59,122 returned as merchants, 30,052 were Jews.

i. In Algiers in 1881 nearly the whole trade was in the hands of the Jews.

4. *A name and a praise* (Zeph. 3:19–20). "Behold, at that time I will undo all that afflict thee: and I will save her that halteth, and gather her that was driven out; and *I will get them praise and fame in every land where they have been put to shame.* At that time will I bring you again even in the time that I gather you: for I will make you a name and a praise among all people of the earth, when I turn back your captivity before your eyes, saith the Lord" (italics mine). Of course the fullness of this prophecy will be realized only in millennial days. But whether there be any connection between the present facts and the prophecy, the facts exist and look very much as though the first drops of that mighty shower of blessing were already beginning to fall upon the Jews.

Fame and a name and a praise do not necessarily follow on emancipation. It has not followed in the case of African-Americans in the United States and in the West Indies, nor in the case of the serfs in Russia.

One of the effects of the emancipation of the Jews was their admission to schools and colleges, and we note the following results:

a. In Berlin recently, out of 3,609 students, 1,302 were Jews.

b. In the high schools of Vienna lately out of 2,488 students, 1,039 were Jews.

c. In Lower Austria recently out of 2,140 advocates, 1,024 were Jews.

d. In Germany the Jews are 1 in 75 of the population but in the German universities the Jews are 1 in 10.

e. In Hungary in 1878-9 the Jews were 4 percent of the population, while in many of the schools they are 75 percent. In the whole kingdom 18 percent of the students at the schools are Jews; 36 percent at the colleges and 25 percent of the faculty of law!

f. We cannot count the names of Jews who are renowned in the literary, educational, and musical worlds. In Berlin out of twenty-three newspapers there are only two not under Jewish control. At a gathering of editors lately in Dresden, 29 out of 43 were Jews. And in Austria at the last census, out of 370 persons who returned themselves as authors, 225 were Jews (nearly two-thirds).

g. In England out of 20,000 clergy of the church of England, 200 are Jews—and thus 1 in 100 Jews are clergymen, as against 1 Gentile in 1,300!

h. In the political world, we cannot enumerate the many names of renown, in all countries, while the number of seats held in various parliaments is out of all proportion compared with the smallness of their numbers to the whole population.

5. *Increase in numbers* (Isa. 60:22). "A little one shall become a thousand, and a small one a strong nation: I the Lord will hasten it in his time"; so also Isaiah 27:6; Jeremiah 31:27 and Ezekiel 36:37. These of course refer to millennial days, but, when we remember how terribly the number of Jews decreased during seventeen centuries, and contrast the wonderful increase in recent years, it seems almost miraculous and certainly leads us to reflect whether these prophecies are not beginning to be fulfilled. For eighteen hundred years God has done as He said He would: "watch over them to destroy and afflict." If this sudden and marvelous change has taken place, has He not ceased to "watch" for this purpose, and begun to "hasten" their increase?

a. In 1708 the Jewish population was estimated at 3 million. Today they are not less than 12 million.

b. In Germany, as to births, the proportion of Jews to Gentiles is as 5.5 to 3.8. And as to longevity, at Frankfort (1846–1858) one quarter of the Gentile population died before reaching 7 years of age, while one-quarter of all the Jews not until 28 1/4 years of age. One-half of all Gentiles born died before reaching 6 years, while one-half of all Jews born survived to 53 years of age. Three-quarters of all Gentiles born died before 60 years of age, but Jews not before 71.

   c. In Prussia (1816–1867) the whole population increased 91 percent, but the Jews 112 percent.

   d. In Austria-Galicia (1820–1870) the population increased 25 percent, but the Jews 150 percent.

6. *Gentile decline.* In Isaiah 33:1; 51:22–23 and Jeremiah 30:10–11, we read that when God thus takes the cup of trembling out of the hand of the Jew, He will put it into the hand of the Gentile. He will also make a full end of the nations whither the Jews have been driven.

What is the principle that has led to Jewish emancipation? *Equality.* What is the principle animating all the present forces of disintegration? *Equality!* This is the very canker which today is beginning to eat into the vitals of the Gentile nations, the that which when driven home, will, split up and break up the nations of the world.

7. *The Jew is to bring this about* as the instrument, see Micah 5:8–9 and Zechariah 12:6.

   a. The Jews are the fathers of modern rationalism in the person of Spinoza and Strauss (see Archdeacon Lee on *Inspiration*, pp. 463–6).

   b. As to socialism, communism, internationalism, nihilism, and anarchy, we read that in 1848, the Jews, Karl Marx, and Karl Leibknecht organized the International Working Men's Association. Marx drew up the laws of the present movement in 1864.

   c. In Germany, a Jew, Ferdinand Lassalle, in 1863 founded the German socialist party. And the textbooks of socialism are Marx's *Critique of Capital*, and Lassalle's *System of Acquired Rights* (arguing that capital is robbery)!

   d. The Russian nihilists have among them ten times as many Jews as of all others put together.[3]

In conclusion, all these things are new. What we now see has not been seen before or until now! It is the beginning of the end! All these facts seem to tell us that many Scriptures are beginning to be fulfilled, and that before long God will remove His heavenly people and deal again, first in judgment and afterward in mercy, with His earthly people Israel.

Restoration can be the only result of all these combined movements. If the Jews are to repossess Palestine, Turkey must lose it. In 1822 Turkey lost Greece. In our day she has lost Romania, Servia (Serbia), Bulgaria, Cyprus, then more of Greece, then Tunis, while Egypt, Armenia, and Arabia are on the move.

The Eastern Question

The Eastern question is the one question with which all the newspapers of Europe are filled, all minds are occupied, and to which all eyes are turned. All the nations of Europe are arming themselves for its settlement, but it will never be settled until God takes it up, and how near may be the time when He will do so we cannot tell. But as we know that summer is near when we see the buds and the leaves, though we know not the day, so we may tell that the time cannot be far distant when God will take up the Eastern question, and with it the Jewish question[4] and settle both forever.

Many circumstances point to it.

1. The equal rights of men call for it.

2. The principle of restoring nationalities call for it. The cry of Germany for the Germans, Italy for the Italians, Greece for the Greeks, and so forth, demand Palestine for the Jews.

3. Jewish movements point to it. The Jewish *Chronicle* (December 17, 1880), says, "We are inundated with books on Palestine, and the air is thick with schemes for colonizing the Holy Land once more."

4. "The Palestine Exploration Fund" has turned the eyes and hearts and thoughts, yes and the feet of thousands of God's servants toward the stones and dust of Emmanuel's

Land, and caused the words of Psalm 102:13–14 to have a new and most solemn and important significance:

> *Thou shalt arise and have mercy upon Zion: for the time to favor her, yea the set time is come. For thy servants take pleasure in her stones and favor the dust thereof.*

Endnotes

1. London, James Nisbet & Co.
2. That is, the day of Jacob's trouble, verse 6.
3. See the *Nineteenth Century* for January 1881. "The dawn of the Revolutionary Epoch."
4. See an important article in the *Century Magazine* for February 1883, entitled "The Jew and the Eastern Question."

Books by E. W. Bullinger

The Book of Job
Bullinger's commentary on the oldest book of the Bible offers a distinctive translation of the book of Job with explanatory notes that follow the literary and critical style of the book. In addition, figures of speech and divine names and titles are given special attention.
ISBN 0-8254-2291-4   218 pp.   paperback

Commentary on Revelation
The pastor, teacher, and serious Bible student will find this book to be both practical and profound. Written in verse-by-verse style, Bullinger devotes major discussions to key problems contained in Revelation.
ISBN 0-8254-2289-2   738 pp.   paperback

The Companion Bible
(Notes and Appendices by E. W. Bullinger) Notes given with the text provide valuable insight into the original Greek and Hebrew languages, as well as alternate translations, explanations of figures of speech, cross references, and detailed introductory outlines of each book and chapter. Additional helps include 198 appendices containing explanations of Hebrew words and their use,

charts, parallel passages, maps, lists of proper names, calendars and timelines. Notes are keyed to these indexes.

ISBN 0-8254-2203-5	2160 pp.	hardcover
ISBN 0-8254-2288-4	2160 pp.	bonded leather
ISBN 0-8254-2237-x	2160 pp.	genuine leather

GREAT CLOUD OF WITNESSES IN HEBREWS ELEVEN
A classic exposition of the great heroes of the faith. Full of rich, practical applications.

ISBN 0-8254-2247-7	462 pp.	paperback

HOW TO ENJOY THE BIBLE
A unique introduction to the study of God's Word. Bullinger guides the reader on an adventure of open and honest study of the Scriptures from the inside out—letting it speak for itself. Believers will be encouraged as they discover how to read, study, and enjoy the Bible.

ISBN 0-8254-2213-2	464 pp.	paperback
ISBN 0-8254-2287-6	464 pp.	deluxe hardcover

NUMBER IN SCRIPTURE
A classic reference book on biblical numerology which provides a complete synopsis of the spiritual significance of numbers found in the Bible.

ISBN 0-8254-2238-8	312 pp.	paperback

WITNESS OF THE STARS
An in-depth study of the constellations and principal stars as they pertain to prophetic truth. More than 40 charts and diagrams are included.

ISBN 0-8254-2245-0	212 pp.	paperback

WORD STUDIES ON THE HOLY SPIRIT
(Foreword by Warren W. Wiersbe) An examination of each of the 385 occurrences of *pneuma* (spirit) in the New

Testament by a great Greek and Hebrew scholar. Includes subject, text, and Greek word indexes.

ISBN 0-8254-2246-9   232 pp.   paperback